Memoirs of a Former Bitter Bitch

Colyn Wanjiru

Printed in the United States of America

ISBN-13: 978-1-7379638-0-6

Dedication

This book is dedicated to my Mama for taking the initial step to break the generational cycles of shame and secrecy by moving to the U.S. to seek her own freedom. Thank you for your blessing of encouraging me to write my story and in doing so revealing your own.

I also dedicate this book to all the resilient little girls and grown women still healing from their childhood traumas. I encourage you to claim your Beauty for Ashes that God promised. Claim your best life through knowledge, forgiveness and faith.

Thank you to every single person who encouraged me through this healing and writing process. All your kind words are deeply appreciated.

Contents

Foreword

Since the idea and title for this memoir came to me and has been sitting in my spirit for the past 30 years, I never really gave thought to what the message was supposed to be. I just knew I was supposed to write it. I knew it would be cathartic for me but also for anyone else who can relate to my story. My story is of a resilient girl who, despite what she was told, decided to pursue her own truth. If I had to sum up the message I want to convey, it comes down to these things: Seek out God for yourself; you will be pleasantly surprised. Fight for your individuality; it is your superpower. Don't be afraid to be authentically you; people respect transparency, and God already knows who you really are anyway. Cycles of trauma and healing are ongoing throughout our lives; spirituality is the only thing that helps us have peace in this process. Life is a journey to find our way back to God.

Part One

How It Began

I started calling myself a "bitter bitch" at the age of 26, as a joke, but somehow the moniker stuck and became my reality. I always said that I would wait until there was an upturn to my permeating bitterness, like a fucking lesson would somehow emerge, and this book could serve as someone's inspiration to achieving a better emotional and spiritual life.

Well, I am 41 years old now, and that epiphany has not yet come, so I said, "Fuck it" and just started writing. I figure at the very least seeing my story unfold on the page will be cathartic for me and entertaining for others to map the roots of my rage. I always promised God that if I was given a platform to share my stories, I wouldn't hold back anything. I want to be fully transparent, so everyone can see how secrecy and shame can be buried so deeply that even I fooled myself into thinking I was fine.

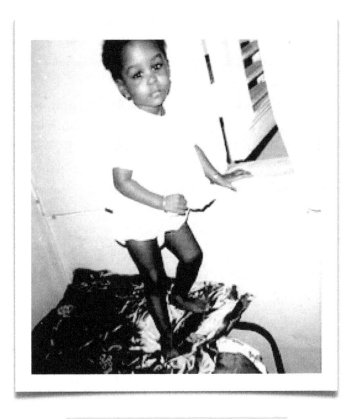

2 years old already looking serious

Chapter One

From Harlem to Trinidad and Back

I guess the only place to start is the beginning. As a matter of fact, even before my birth, the drama was preordained by some tea leaf reader at a party my mother went to in Trinidad.

She told my mother that the child she was carrying would be a great person one day. I always wondered what the hell that meant because to this day, "Life for me ain't been no crystal stair," to quote the great Langston Hughes.

As I studied the lives of bonafide great people, I saw no similarities. In fact, I thought everyone achieved their greatness before their 35th birthday. I was relieved when I hit 36 years old because I did not really expect to live long past that birthday.

Not that I have lived my life particularly recklessly, but I have always had a vivid imagination, believing that I would die in some dramatic fashion in some spiritual tug of war with demons battling for my soul. Yeah, I am the original drama queen!

Honestly, I have always been drawn to supernatural things, mainly for power, because I felt so lonely and weak as a child.

Plus, shit just seems to happen to me! Let me go back to the earliest days that I remember… my years in Trinidad before I came to the United States when I was around three years old.

I must have been impatient to get my life started because I didn't even wait for the full term to be born. I came out two months early at three pounds on December 11, 1966. My mother was a 23-year-old illegal Trinidadian immigrant, Atlanta Isabel Downes. I came into the world at 10:00 p.m. in the most flavorful city in the world, New York City, Harlem hospital, to be exact. She must have known something was up from then because she named me the most androgynous name on earth… Colyn Stacy Birchwood. On paper, I looked like an Englishman.

Mama was naïve but determined to raise me alone in cold- ass New York City. Birchwood was the surname of the dude she married to stay in America. Yeah, illegal immigration was rampant back then, too. She would make up a few lies throughout my early years regarding who my real father was. For years she told me that she didn't know who he was and that she was raped at a party.

When I finally questioned her about why she kept me, she said she didn't personally believe in abortions. I think my question shook her, but she stuck to the story until I was a grown woman. Mama later apologized and admitted she was ashamed of getting played by my father, who turned out to be married. She wouldn't even admit to my Granny who he was, but fate has a way of catching up to you.

* * *

Mama came to the United States to get away from her abusive and controlling upbringing and to get as far away from Granny as possible. Unfortunately, my health would send her right back to Trinidad to keep me alive.

Being illegal and needing to keep a job to support now two mouths in the dead of winter, my mother went back to work about two weeks after I was born. She was a hospital administrator at Mount Sinai Hospital in Manhattan. While she was at work, I was left with a babysitter in the neighborhood. One night when I was about three months old, Mama returned to pick me up and found me having trouble breathing. The sitter had placed my bassinet on the radiator for warmth. I guess this was the ghetto version of turning the heat up.

I was born with respiratory problems from being premature, and the dry heat caused my breathing to be labored. I also had asthma and bronchitis. Basically, my life was in danger already! Mama rushed me to the hospital on foot during a blizzard, and the doctors saved me. However, the weather was proving to be a detriment to my health, so Mama had to ask Granny if she would raise me in Trinidad because the climate was more conducive to improving my respiratory ailments.

Despite their turbulent relationship, Granny agreed to take me in to live with her and Auntie May down on 7 Borde Street in Port of Spain, Trinidad.

As my Granny would tell me later, she immediately knew who my father was when she saw me. Trinidad is an island at the Southern end of the Caribbean, and families often know each other just like in American small towns.

Apparently, I was the spitting image of my father, John Cayonne. He was a playwright, actor, and performer who had moved to Toronto to do theater. Granny knew of his reputation as a player/womanizer and disapproved of my mother seeing him...clearly for good reason. When my mother told him of her pregnancy, he gave her money for an illegal abortion and had nothing more to do with her. Being the proud and stubborn woman she was, Mama severed her ties with him, too.

* * *

I spent my first three years of life in a household with values based upon English customs, class divisions, and strict Anglican religion. Granny and I bonded from day one because she had a quick wit and a stoic demeanor that, for some reason, always intrigued me. As stern as she could be with others, she could never stay stern with me. I always had a knack for breaking through her cold exterior with my playfulness.

I don't really remember bonding with Auntie May in the same way because she was always sickly. She suffered with complications from diabetes and respiratory ailments which kept her mostly housebound. Auntie May was a former schoolteacher, and education was revered in our house, much like most Caribbean families.

She taught me as a toddler to read fluently by having me memorize the alphabet chart out in this little shed in the yard. It was our makeshift schoolhouse for me and my 5-year-old cousin, Avril.

My Sundays were spent entertaining Granny and her friends by reading the newspaper for them and showing them I could bow and curtsey, in case I ever met the Queen, I guess. I also performed the latest American dances that I would see on TV.

Mama used to send me Jackson 5 records from the States. I always loved to imitate Michael Jackson's singing and kept up with the latest dances. Music and dancing were always my outlets, like it was literally in my blood.

* * *

Our house was considered modern by Trinidad standards in those days because we had indoor plumbing, a television, a piano, and a telephone. Many folks had outside showers and no electrical appliances. I remember thinking we were rich because Granny always instilled that in me. She taught me about class and "keeping to my own kind," which basically meant that I couldn't play with the "ruffian" children that rented the back house from her.

Even my own cousins were considered low-class to Granny because they lived in Laventille, which is the equivalent of the Port of Spain hood. Granny looked down on them because I guess she figured they did not spend their inheritance well. In her mind, anything European and proper was considered acceptable, basically like "white is right." They were living in the shantytown amongst the common folks, which to Granny was unheard of.

My great-grandfather, Charles Hubert Downes, was a stowaway from Barbados who landed in Trinidad around

1889. He arrived on the docks and worked his way up from a train porter to become the head of the Trinidad railroad. He amassed a fortune by becoming a moneylender and purchasing large amounts of real estate.

At the height of his dominance, he owned a healthy amount of commercial and residential real estate in downtown Port of Spain. Pappy, as he was called by his daughters, did not allow Granny or her sisters to work or marry; he controlled them with his money.

When I read V.C. Andrews' Flowers in the Attic, it always reminded me of my family history. The stoic appearance of the proper upbringing, but with an ever-present air of loneliness and dark secrets. Ironically enough, since she never worked a day in her life, Granny never replenished the wealth that her father had built up. In her later years, all that she considered grand had to be sold to keep up with her lifestyle.

* * *

Two major things that I remember about my early childhood are my vivid imagination and my stubborn nature. I remember I used to suck my thumb and carry a blanket, just like Linus from Peanuts, until I was at least seven years old. Granny tried to break me of that habit with many methods; of course, spanking was the first one.

That shit never worked, so she had to try those old school home remedies. She put pepper sauce on my thumb before I went to sleep, and in the morning she would be disgusted because I just licked that shit off and kept on sucking. She even tried to wrap my thumb up in a bandage and pin my arm to my chest so I couldn't get to it, but that didn't work either.

Finally, I guess she just decided to let me do me. Back in the day, I was always a light eater; as a matter of fact, I didn't even like to eat at all. (Damn, I wish I could go back to that mindset!)

Granny would give me porridge or any type of food, and I would let that dish get cold, thinking I could wait her out. We would have a serious stalemate; she would tell me that I couldn't get up until I finished, and I would sit there and stubbornly not eat. I would always win. Sometimes it would be afternoon before she would let me get up from the table. To this day, I like my food at room temperature.

The only food that I always loved was bread and anything dairy-related. My favorite time was tea time. Granny would have proper tea and biscuits before bed in the good old English tradition, and I absolutely loved that shit. The tea was extra sweet, and the bread was homemade, or we ate some good butter crackers with REAL butter and real cheese.

We even ate glucose powder, called KLIM every night… yet more sugar, probably embedding diabetes into my DNA. Granny often baked cakes from scratch, and sometimes she would put rose flavoring in them. Definitely the start of my love affair with anything rich and cholesterol-laden.

* * *

I remember one Sunday playing in the drawing-room while Granny was in the dining room entertaining friends after supper. I had been eyeing the electric socket for a while, and I remember her telling me not to touch it… which of course to me meant TOUCH IT… that shit was calling my name!

Man, I stuck my finger in that socket, and it knocked me back a couple of inches on my ass! When I looked at Granny and started to cry, she just gave me that steely look and said in her low deep voice, with absolutely no sympathy, "I told you not to touch it, and you better not cry." So, I just held my finger and sobbed silently. This was my first lesson in suppressing my emotions at age two.

* * *

While I was in Trinidad, Mama came to visit me often. Although I don't recall either her or Granny being affectionate, she would always bring me gifts. In particular, I remember a doll that I had named Sally that was supposed to walk and talk. I never liked that Sally because it seemed too damned independent for a doll. It was almost as big as me, brown-skinned, and I couldn't figure out how that damn doll walked.

I also had a Slinky and was scared of that, too. How the hell does a metal object keep on moving down the steps when you let it go? That shit freaked me out. I guess that was evidence of my active imagination.

Although Trinidad is known for the greatest Carnival celebration in the world, I was not allowed to participate because Carnival's origin was from the devil, according to Granny. Carnival literally means a celebration of decadence and "bacchanal" before you go into the 40 days of fasting and Lenten observance beginning on Ash Wednesday. Basically,

Carnival begins around Sunday night and everyone drinks, parties, and plays "mas" until Tuesday or J'ouvert morning. It is when all inhibitions are released, and Eurocentric traditions of suppressing sexuality are rebelled against. Playing "Mas" is slang for dressing up and masquerading as folk characters representing various Caribbean cultural origins. The costumes range from the scandalous "skin- out" strips of material barely covering the most private body parts to the dark and ominous homages to the spirit world.

I remember leaning over the gate and peering down the street at the costumed revelers. It was both scary and intriguing at the same time. I was drawn to the bright colors of the costumes and the music, yet frightened by the "moko jumbies" and demonic masks that some folks wore. This may have been the jump-off to my interest in all things considered taboo.

When not in the throes of Carnival bacchanal, Trinidad has a pretty laid-back atmosphere with the emphasis on living life to the fullest or "liming," as Trinis say. It also has a strong Anglican Church tradition, which the English colonizers brought to the country.

However, Trinidad is also known for the diverse cultural backgrounds infused into the society by other races of settlers besides Africans. East Indian and Chinese foods and customs are a part of Trinidadian culture as are West African and European customs. Although Granny did not really socialize with other races, I was very aware of their presence. I was never aware of any racial tension at that age. I never really saw any white people either.

Overall, this early period of my life was really the easiest part. Despite Granny's strict discipline, it was the norm for me, and it was the only life that I knew. I never really interacted with other children my age, yet I didn't miss it.

When I learned to read, I began to find solace and companionship in books. Back then, the standard reading material for little kids was Dick and Jane books or Little Sambo books. I remember reading, "See Dick run. See Spot run. See Jane play." I didn't recognize the inherent racism of the Little Sambo books with the caricature of the African savage boy with the huge red lips or the Indian boy swinging in the damn jungle.

The Sambo characters were interchangeable between the two races; the commonality was the savageness. I never really wondered why none of the folks in the books looked like me. I had all of the same material stuff that the kids in the book had, except for the traditional family structure, so I guess I never questioned the omission of Black kids.

Granny was into quality, "sturdy" products like Bata shoes and leather school bags...anything that was deemed upper class or European. In Trinidad, the custom is to buy gold jewelry for kids, once again, I guess to show class and proper upbringing. I had the gold bangles, earrings, frilly dresses, cute little frocks, and my hair was done with the little ribbons and stuff... real feminine. Granny started me off right, bless her heart...

* * *

Mama's best friend, Auntie Rhona, visited me when she would travel back to Trinidad to see her family. When I was about 3 years old, we went out when she came down, and we went somewhere where there was a long staircase. I guess being raised by older women caused me to act like them, old and cautious. So, I was always afraid of stuff, like walking down the stairs one at a time. I would only go to the next step after I rested on each step with both of my feet. I guess other habits that I had were reminiscent of old folks, too. So, she went back and reported to my mother that it was time for me to come live with her in the States.

Granny and I were both devastated because that was the only family that I knew, and I am sure that I was refreshing to their lives. As Granny put it, "Your mother sent you to me all sickly and at death's door. Now that I have raised you and gave you a good foundation, she want to come and take you back!"

Plans were made for me to return home with Mama at a later date. One of the last memories I have of Trinidad was my Auntie Dorothy dying. Auntie D was the party girl of the 3 Downes sisters. She got pregnant out of wedlock and was sent away to family in Barbados to have the baby. She rebelled against Pappy, took her inheritance, and bought a small property in Laventille, where she lived with her daughter Margaret.

Pappy never allowed his daughters to marry the men they chose for themselves; they were never good enough for him. Unfortunately, this would seal their fate of becoming spinsters. Back in the day and especially in a society so dominated by sexist European customs, independent women were considered "rebellious." Basically, if you didn't have a man, you were worthless. Auntie D ignored that stigma and still did "her."

I never really knew her that well because she didn't come around that often, but she was always laughing and very pleasant. Once she moved into Laventille, she was considered common, and that did not sit well with upper class Granny. I answered the door one day, and it was Auntie D. When she came in, she was holding her throat, and Granny brought her some Milo to drink.

She was complaining of not being able to keep anything down. When she drank the Milo, it came out of her nose and mouth. Apparently, she had some type of cancerous tumor in her throat. The next thing I remember is her being rushed to Port of Spain General Hospital and Granny and Auntie May crying.

After that, I remember her coffin laid out in the drawing room and people quietly paying their respects and filing through the house. I guess it was practical to have the wake at the house because the cemetery with the family burial plot was right across the street. I was aware that she was not coming back, and it all seemed so sudden to me... I first saw her smiling face, and then she was gone.

We were right across from Lapeyrouse Cemetery in Woodbrook, and I'm sure this has a little something to do with my crazy fear of the dark. Back in the day, wakes and funerals were held in the house. You know I was traumatized by that! I always felt that perhaps I saw spirits or heard them or something because, basically, I am terrified of the dark and can't figure out why.

I don't remember ever sleeping alone while living there;

I was either sharing a bed with Granny or my Auntie May. When I got older, I visited my Granny about a year before she passed, and I took my buddy Rico with me.

Rico is sensitive to spirits, and after our first night there, he slept in my Auntie May's old room, where she had passed away in 1978. He told me that he could not sleep because of all the spirits coming back and forth into the room to look at him.

I was surprised but relieved that they didn't bother with me, or at least I didn't see them. Living across from the cemetery, I guess they didn't have far to travel home.

* * *

Although Mama and Auntie D were very close, Granny never told her that Auntie D had died until after the funeral. For some reason, she did not find it necessary for Mama to return from the States for that event. This definitely exaggerated the resentment toward Granny that Mama already had. She came down to take me away soon after that. I left Trinidad for New York City when I was about 4.

Mama roomed with Auntie Rhona in a small apartment in Harlem on 125th Street. Auntie Rhona was a hotel catering manager, and Mama still worked in hospital administration. While she was at work, I was sent to Morningside Day Care, where my teachers were…believe it or not, Ms. Lemon and Ms. Ham. To me, they looked just like their names. Ms. Lemon was tall and thin and light-skinned, with her hair in a bun, and Mrs. Ham was a little plump and brown-skinned. They also reminded me physically of my Granny and Auntie May, so that was a bit comforting in my new social environment of public school.

It didn't take long for my differences to become apparent to the teachers. Back then, all the kids went to the bathroom at the same time in one big facility, with the boys peeing on one side and the girls on the other, but it was all open, so we could see one another.

I remember being adamant that I wanted to stand up and face forward to pee like the boys. I was so serious about this that Mama was told about it when she came to pick me up from school that day. She tried to explain to me, like the teachers did, that girls don't pee like that, and I had to follow the teachers' instructions. I went along with it, but I sure didn't like it.

* * *

Around that time is when I also discovered that I preferred boys' clothes over dresses and skirts. Back in Trinidad, I was never dressed in pants because it was hot, and girls just didn't really do that. However, winter in NYC is no joke, so corduroy pants and jeans and sweaters were more practical than fashionable. Once I discovered pants, I was good!

Mama tried to hook me up with the frilly panties and skirts, but I couldn't wait to get home and put on my comfortable "play clothes." These consisted of some corduroys with knee patches and my favorite red Donald Duck sweatshirt with the quacking, googly-eyed appliqué on the front.

* * *

Living with my mother as an only child during that period was such a peaceful time in my life, and we really bonded. Mama was about 26, slim, naturally beautiful, with a stunning smile, caramel complexion, hazel eyes, melodic accent, and confident attitude. I always admired how she carried herself very regally.

She usually wore a short Afro, with beautiful African style earrings and accessories. Mama loved shoes, fashion, books, music, and culture. She would always be sharply dressed to go to work or hang out with her friends on the weekends.

Our evenings were spent listening to music of all kinds while she cooked homemade Trini style meals; Mama was into rice and beans of all kinds. Again, adding to the layers of my love affair with food. To this day, I still love stewed lentils or channa, and a good red beans and rice will make my toes curl.

Her love of varied styles of music was infused into me as well. I grew up listening to everything from African Highlife and Afro-Cuban jazz to traditional calypso, parang, and reggae to Pop and classical. Artists like Nancy Wilson, Miriam Makeba, Hugh Masekela, Al Hirt, Grover Washington, Lou Rawls, even Percy Sledge and Burt Bacharach were Mama's favorites. She taught me how to limbo under a broomstick in the kitchen and how to "whine" off of the old Harry Belafonte and Lord Kitchener records. Whining is the traditional hip swaying and pelvic thrusting dance done throughout the Caribbean to calypso and soca music. It's really a rite of passage for many kids. Although whining appears very sexualized, I was never taught it was anything but natural rhythmic movement.

Mama had a very operatic voice, soprano with a lot of vibratto, and loved to sing. She taught me old Trinidadian folk songs, like "Brown Gyal in the Ring." Real facts, she actually owned the record, "Put the Lime in the Coconut," performed by some 60s ukulele playing beach trio.

Mama also loved authentic, by New York standards, Chinese food. She would take me to her favorite restaurants in Chinatown, where we would share soup and roast pork dumplings. The restaurant had a mechanical dragon that would come out of its lair and roar and send off sparks when you put money in the slot.

One of my other favorite activities with Mama was shoe shopping. We used to go to the Buster Brown store on 125th, and she would let me ride the mechanical fire engine when we finished trying on shoes. So many of my wonderful childhood memories of New York and Mama revolve around food, music, and shopping. Before the bitterness set in.

Mama did like to go out to get her dance on, and her friends would come over to the apartment to get ready to go out after work. I would always love to stand behind them in the bathroom and watch them put their makeup on.

Mama's friend Auntie Gloria would always say, "We have a little admirer here." I would be grinning like a kid in a candy store. Even back then, I was enamored with pretty women. I never desired to BE LIKE them when I grew up as they thought; I just loved looking at all that beauty. I didn't know what the attraction was called, but I knew I always wanted to be surrounded by beautiful women. I also loved the affection and attention I got from them.

Mama was never all that physically affectionate. She didn't like all that touching and stuff. When I got the chickenpox, she told me I had to stay away from her because it was contagious, so I made sure to run and hug and kiss her on purpose because I knew she didn't like it. Of course, she caught the pox and was quarantined with me for a week.

Another thing I discovered about Mama around that time was that she wasn't the type to do well in a crisis. She would panic and get squeamish. I was always an adventurous kid, and I loved to test the limits with EVERYTHING. So naturally, when I discovered orifices on my body could be filled with things, I tried.

I loved oranges, and one day I got the idea to see if the seed could fit up my nose. I pushed it up too far, and it got stuck. I ran to Mama so she could get it out because I was getting scared, but she got all panicked, screaming, not doing anything to help the situation.

Thank God Auntie Rhona was home, and she slapped my back so hard the seed flew across the room. You would think that the electric socket scare would have turned me off of experimentation, but nope.

* * *

I also loved to taste things…actually, I wanted to know what EVERYTHING tasted like. I ate dirt, boogers, ear wax, got my tongue stuck on cold metal, tasted the seatbelts in the car and on the plane, licked the pole on the subway. I loved to taste the different soaps and lotions, especially the good-smelling kind. I guess I was an extra inquisitive kid.

Back then, people were not so indulgent with their kids, and, basically, whatever was put in front of you, you were expected to eat. Mama was on a budget, and she had bought one of those packs of cereal that included Grape Nuts in the lineup.

We got down to the last box of cereal in the pack, which was the nasty Grape Nuts, aka twigs and berries. Since I was being forced to eat it, I decided to spice it up a bit by adding my own condiments.

I mixed sugar, salt, ketchup, and toothpaste on the cereal, and, of course, that shit was disgusting, to put it mildly. Mama made me eat that shit because she said I was wasting her food. I cut back on my experimentation a bit after that.

* * *

One quality Mama always had was a strong sense of duty and responsibility and good money management. She always had a good job with benefits and excellent work ethics. Because of this, she was able to keep abreast of my healthcare needs.

I was born cross-eyed and needed to have surgery to correct the condition at age 4. I am always grateful that she had the presence of mind to get me the surgery every time I see someone with the Aaliyah eye patch. Being born with vision problems, I had to wear glasses quite early in life. I wore glasses before I even started kindergarten.

* * *

While employed at Mount Sinai Hospital, Mama's boss was a wonderful older Jewish woman named Isabel Asch, "Aunt Isabel" to me. She became Mama's benefactor and sponsor so she could become a citizen. I think what sealed their bond was that they shared Isabel, Mama's middle name.

She also took an immediate liking to me and would take me out on cultural outings in Manhattan. She was instrumental in developing my love of the arts by taking me to events that Mama could not always afford. Aunt Isabel was my introduction to the finer material things in life. She spoke to me like I was an adult, and she always encouraged my intellect and curiosity.

She lived in a large two-bedroom apartment on Central Park West that just screamed old money. I even enjoyed taking the subway ride to her house because the atmosphere was so different from Harlem. After you passed the 116th Street stop and the Columbia University students would board the train, from then on, the faces on the train would get lighter and more diverse.

Her stop was 81st Street, directly across from the famous Museum of Natural History and the Hayden Planetarium. From the very beginning, I took to the bourgeois life like a fish to water. Her building had a doorman, and an elevator man who operated the manual elevator.

She had a maid and a cook to prepare the food delivered to her door, which was quite expensive back in the 70s. This was my first experience with someone who had servants, and they were very respectful of me.

Her husband, John Asch, was an author whose claim to

fame was that he was the relative of a famous Jewish author, Chaim Potok. Their apartment was tastefully decorated with antique wood furniture, real Persian rugs and handmade tapestries, original oil paintings, and various ethnic artifacts from her travels to Israel and Europe.

Although not spacious, her kitchen was equipped with all the appliances of the day like a toaster oven, KitchenAid mixer, a manual juicer, fine china and crystal, and real silverware. I had not seen dishes like that except in my Granny's house. Although she clearly had wealth, she was never ostentatious; but instead, she was quite generous.

Her fashions and jewelry were impeccable. She had wonderful heirloom pieces of jewelry in all types of precious stones. Her shoes were mostly Ferragamo, Gucci, Aigner, and other Italian designers. Throughout the years, she taught me about quality fashion versus trendy styles.

Aunt Isabel was very indulgent in ways Mama was not, or probably could not afford to be. She added to my already burgeoning love of food by introducing me to international cuisine and name brand food products.

Since Mama was on a tight budget, we pretty much had store brand groceries or the cheaper name brand only if it was on sale. With Aunt Isabel, I was introduced to fresh-squeezed orange juice, real maple syrup imported from Vermont, and real Danish oatmeal. Until then, I had no idea that simple pancake syrup was just thickened sugar water and Quaker was not real oats!

We dined at the finest Italian, Indian, and Chinese restaurants in Manhattan. She taught me how to understand the menus by deciphering the ingredients in the dishes. She would ask me if I liked cheese or tomatoes or a type of meat and then explain what was in the dish in question.

She also encouraged me to ask the waiter questions about the dish if I did not understand how it was made. Our deal was if I ordered it, I had to eat it, and I was always ready to comply with that.

She always made me feel that my opinion mattered by just engaging me in normal conversation about anything, despite my young age. Whenever she discovered that I enjoyed something, she would always make it available when I visited. To this day, I can't eat any more 3 Musketeers bars because she would let me have them literally until I became nauseous.

Since she did live across from the Museum of Natural History, I saw the dinosaur exhibit quite a few times. We also visited the Metropolitan Museum of Art and Lincoln Center for various musical performances.

New York is such a collage of culture and varied forms of performance art, and we took it all in. My favorite outings with her were during the Christmas season. Although Aunt Isabel was Jewish, she would take me to Rockefeller Center every year to see the Christmas tree and Radio City Music Hall to see the Christmas show.

We would stroll down 5th Avenue and look at all the wonderfully decorated stores. I would especially love going to FAO Schwarz to see the humongous stuffed animals. These animals were the characters in my children's books, like Curious George and The Cat in the Hat. They had a

Paddington the Bear that was at least 7 feet tall! We watched the folks ice skating at Rockefeller Center.

We would see whatever Christmas movie was playing at the Guild 50th Street Theater. The best part was seeing the world famous Rockettes up close and personal in all of their pageantries. Aunt Isabel had a niece who was a ballerina with the NYC Ballet. When I got a little older, about 7 years old, we incorporated seeing The Nutcracker every Christmas into our outings. Honestly, the times with Aunt Isabel became an oasis of peace in a life of turmoil.

Chapter Two

Njoroge The Kenyan Svengali

When I was about 4 ½, back in 1971, Mama began dating a Kenyan man named Njoroge. She was 28, and he told her he was 33. Actually, he was quite a bit older than that since there were no written birth records back when he was born in rural Kenya. He was from a province outside of Nairobi called Banana Hill. His father was the head of one of the clans of the Kikuyu tribe. Back in Kenya, his family was kind of a big deal.

He was a Black history professor at City College of New York (CCNY) with a slew of alphabet letters after his name. I'm not sure how long she dated him before introducing him to me. Still, I distinctly remember the first conversation we had, and I was so confused afterward. He and Mama were about to go out, and he came over and introduced himself.

He bent down to my level and was a bit condescending as he said, "My name is Njoroge Chege, and I am going to be marrying your mother." Mama was standing behind him, grinning and nodding her head, while he further explained to me that he was going to adopt me and become my father.

He also informed me that I would no longer be Colyn

Stacy Birchwood; I would now be Wanjiru Chege. I guess my mother held on to the Colyn because my birth certificate was changed to Colyn Wanjiru wa Chege, the "wa" meaning I now belonged to Chege.

I was officially part of the Kenyan Chege family, whether I liked it or not. I was devastated; I loved my name Colyn because it was a part of my Granny's name.

Mama told me that she wanted to honor my grandmother by naming me after her, but she never liked the name Ethelyn, so she settled on Colyn. Not sure where the Stacy came in, but I liked that too. I would use that as my "club name" later in life to stay connected to it.

* * *

The way they both hit me with that news was a bit jarring. I went from having a pronounceable name, to which I related, to having a name to which I felt no connection; the only saving grace was that Njoroge told me the legend of Wanjiru and how she was a great princess and was one of the daughters of Father God that lived on Mt. Kenya.

He also told me that the name meant generous, so I really liked that quality, and I warmed up to the name quickly. I haven't been able to verify that definition anywhere. However, I still claim it, which kept me from hating my name altogether since I grew to hate him.

* * *

The fable of Wanjiru is the story of a beautiful, much sought after girl in the Hills, whose laughter and beautiful smile charmed everyone she encountered. In her father's absence, she was sold to an ogre through his trickery. He disguised himself as a handsome prince, but he revealed his true nature of being an ogre and his ultimate desire to eat her after they were married.

I find this story ironic because that is exactly who Njoroge Chege turned out to be, an ogre who plotted to destroy my mind and self-worth, along with Mama's.

* * *

Initially, I was intrigued by Njoroge; he seemed charming and cavalier. Since I was an avid reader, I was impressed by his massive collection of books on all types of African and Black history, his textbooks, and just his clutter of scholastic material in general. I absolutely loved those little blue exam booklets, with the college-ruled lines, that he brought home to grade with the CCNY official crest on the cover and his impressive title, Dr./Professor John N. Chege, Ph.D. M. Ed.

I was a sucker for a beautiful mind, even as a child. He had a revolutionary spirit, which I also admired; he told me that he had been a part of the Kenyan Mau Mau revolution as a soldier fighting for his country's independence from the British colonizers.

Both he and my mother made me learn the African diaspora's history at a young age as extra homework. I was always a rebel, and the concept of slavery and classism never sat well with me as soon as I learned what it was.

As much as I grew to despise Njoroge, I still appreciate the valuable lessons in pride that he taught me. He was definitely an arrogant man, a Sagittarius like myself, and unapologetic about his education.

Although I had spent my young life enjoying the androgyny of my birth name, Colyn Stacy, once my name was legally changed after he adopted me, I grew to like Wanjiru. He primarily encouraged me to take pride in Pan Africanism, and he never allowed me to be called by any nickname.

He used to tell me, "Your name is only 3 syllables. If they can say Jennifer, they can say Wan-Ji-Ru. You know how Americans always want to dumb names down like it's too hard to pronounce more than one syllable at a time." At first, it annoyed me, the refusal to allow me a nickname.

Still, secretly, I began to admire his demand because I did realize how dismissive it was for teachers to dumb down my name.

* * *

So, I'm kinda fuzzy on the time frame, but at first, Mama and I still lived in our Harlem apartment with her best friend, Auntie Rhona, while she was first dating Njoroge. Those were still sort of fun times, but I could sense the mood changing.

After a few months, I guess, we moved into his apartment a little further up by City College, and my bedroom was his study. I slept surrounded by all those books and newspapers that I found fascinating. This is when the atmosphere started to become a bit more sinister and controlling.

Mama and Njoroge married at the courthouse in Manhattan with me and a couple of Njoroge's friends as witnesses. I remember we came back to the apartment with guests, and we were all sitting in the living room, laughing and talking.

Njoroge asked my mother to do something, and I guess she didn't move fast enough, so he hauled off and slapped her to the floor on their wedding day in full view of all the guests. No one rushed to help or to stop him. We were all stunned, and pretty soon, the party broke up, and Mama was left to nurse her physical and emotional wounds.

I was furious and tried to come to her aid, but she told me it was OK and to go to my room. Right then and there, I started plotting to kill Njoroge. At 5 years old, I became someone with murderous intent, and I was dead-ass serious.

I wondered why my mother stayed with him after that first incident; even I knew it was a precursor of worse to come. A few months later, I found out exactly why... she was pregnant with my sister Wanjiku, who was born in January of 1972.

Apparently Mama had dated him in 1967 briefly but broke it off with him. She ran into him at some Pan-African party, and they hooked up which resulted in her pregnancy. She felt that she had to marry him because she already had me out of wedlock and she was scared of Granny's judgment, further entrenching the cycle of shame surrounding all the "illegitimate" babies in our family. Mama told me how Granny hid her own pregnancy until finally Mama was born in the house and everyone heard her crying. She was never allowed out of the house in the daytime; Granny took her out in the moonlight to avoid the whispers of nosey neighbors. It is so infuriating how the women and children have to bear the shame, and somehow the fathers get off scott free. The kids get hidden like it was their fault for being the product of their parents bad decisions, and the mothers feel that they have to hold on to any piece of man to legitimize their motherhood. Anyway, back to the story…

Clearly, she was pregnant when she agreed to get married, and since Njoroge was willing to adopt her child, who wasn't his, she figured he must be a good man. That slap to the face was like the clanging of jail doors once they close shut. We were trapped in that hateful situation indefinitely.

* * *

Another violent situation that I can never forget was when Njoroge put Mama's head through the painted-over glass on the bathroom door. I don't know what preceded that raging outburst, other than the ever-present liquor and, honestly, just his cruel nature. Until that day, I had no idea that the bathroom door wasn't wood.

Despite my efforts to suppress this memory, I can still remember my Mother picking glass out of her Afro and me being terrified that he would kill her. She was screaming and saying, "What you want to kill me, nuh?"

This all happened while she was pregnant, too. He didn't give a damn about that. I think this was about when I regressed back to wetting the bed, which I didn't stop until probably around 14 years old. I never realized the connection of bedwetting to fear of the parents until I did some psychology studies later in life. I just know that ass whippings followed after every incident, more to add to my already mounting stressors.

When my sister was born, she came out very light-skinned and red in the face. I remember Njoroge beating Mama because he thought the baby couldn't be his because of her light complexion.

Luckily, she darkened up in a few weeks and displayed some of his Kenyan features, or else that would have been a new problem for Mama. As I write this, I wonder if parents know how deeply these incidents of violence affect their children. For some reason, so many adults don't think that the kids will remember. Trust me, we do.

Still, unfortunately, I think that shit seeps into your soul forever. When the HBO show "Dexter" came out, it depicted how two serial killer brothers were made because they watched their Mother get beaten to death in front of them.

Now that I know a little about psychology, I thank God that my life didn't take a different turn because I was so capable of murder at that young age. And the rage kept building. The bitter roots kept forming.

Njoroge's violent demons were triggered by alcohol, and it showed early on that this was going to be a problem. While we were still living in Harlem, I remember going with Mama to pick him up from a bar because he was too drunk to make it home on his own. I remember the smell of cheap-ass Ballantine beer and that Johnny Walker Red he chose when he wanted to act up.

I still remember seeing him passed out drunk in the living

room wearing his untidy whiteys and wondering what the hell my beautiful Mother was doing with this uncouth brute. And that she still married him after all these red flags.

Chapter Three

Moving on Up to the Bronx

Once my sister was born, we needed a larger apartment, so we moved up to a 3 bedroom 10th floor apartment on Theriot Avenue in the Bronx. The neighborhood was nestled between Parkchester, Castle Hill, and Soundview with a view of the Whitestone Bridge connecting Queens in the distance.

It became quickly evident once we moved into our new high rise in the working middle class section of the Bronx that we were apparently "Movin' on Up" like the Jeffersons. No maid – though we were about to get someone to fill that role – but I'll get to that soon enough. I'm not sure if Mama was ever in love or she just felt obligated, as women tended to do in her generation.

I think that Njoroge, being the Svengali that he was, painted a great picture of how much better life would be. However, once it degenerated into the pit of abuse it really was, she was in too deep and too ashamed and isolated to ask for a way out.

* * *

Njoroge was always the advocate of excellent education, and he took the reins quickly when it came to mine. As soon as we settled into the apartment, he enrolled me in PS 100 right up the street from our building. Although I was only 5 years old, I read fluently at a high school grade level, so he pushed for me to be challenged by skipping to a higher grade. So, I was like the Black girl version of Young Sheldon, 5 years old in the 2nd grade. Academically challenging, yes, but socially challenging, even more so.

I don't regret one bit of my school years, but I must say that it definitely honed my street smarts at an early age. I learned soon enough from my peers that being smart didn't earn me any cool points with my classmates. What did gain their friendship was being quick-witted and snapping on kids to keep them off your ass. If you could make people laugh without embarrassing them enough to kick your ass, you were tolerated.

Since I was so young and tiny, I had a few girls look out for me. They lived in Monroe projects across the street from the school. Since I was never in a rush to get home, I made the trek through the pissy elevators and broken bottle strewn courtyards to visit them after school until my Mama put a stop to it.

Although I realized early that Njoroge was more controlling than a loving father, he always confused me with his periodic bursts of compassion and demonstrations of interest in me. One example I remember happened not too long after I started the 2nd grade, in the lunchroom. As I said, I was probably the youngest and smallest in stature in the whole grade because of my age.

In the middle of lunch, while we were sitting at the long tables with the benches on either side, a fight broke out. While everyone was scrambling to get out of the way, the table flipped over, and I got my finger caught underneath it. The force of the table split my finger at the top, and I needed emergency stitches. I really can't believe it wasn't broken.

The school called Mama, and she and Njoroge came to pick me up. Mama was so freaked out by the sight of the blood that she was hysterical. I remember looking at her like, "WTH?! You're supposed to be the adult and stay calm in this situation." So, Njoroge took me to the emergency room and gave me the "you're a big girl" pep talk, so I could handle the pain of the stitches. I felt a little close to him at that moment, like maybe he wasn't so bad after all. That was short-lived, though.

* * *

So, although we weren't allowed to celebrate Christmas outright, we still did the traditional things like go to friends' houses on the actual holiday to eat and socialize. Njoroge abhorred anything related to white Jesus, but he definitely participated in the alcohol traditions. This eventually led to us getting Christmas gifts because we received them from all of the other friends whose homes we visited.

Anyway, I distinctly remember one year. When I was about 8 years old, I stayed up all night on Christmas Eve to help Njoroge put together a big wheel and tricycle for my siblings. By then, my brother Chege was born. Again, one of those times, I felt close to him, like we were bonding.

And then on Christmas morning, I got a used cheerleader baton from the flea market he worked at. I was so hurt and felt so betrayed because it was like no matter how minimal my requests were, he and my mother found a way to cheapen it even further. Like I wasn't worth anything more than the cheapest version of what I requested.

I know I asked for a bike and some music. I always asked for music or a book. Why the fuck would I even want a damn baton? I wasn't in any band, and I damn sure wasn't a cheerleader, so there was literally no thought of my wants when choosing this present. None. Life went on, and the anger kept building...

* * *

So, as I said before, music and the library were my refuges. Since I read at a high school level at the age of 5, I graduated from the Beverly Cleary and Nancy Drew books rather quickly. I always say it's dangerous to let smart kids loose in the library with no supervision.

I discovered the urban adult books and romance novels way too early to even know how twisted some of those stories were. I remember during summer vacations and school breaks, I would sneak and read Mama's romance novels and quickly skip to the parts that made me tingly.

One of my favorite series was the Iceberg Slim books and Donald Goines tales of pimps and hoes and that dark, seedy hustler life in the Bronx and 42nd Street in NYC. I don't know why but I idolized that pimp life, and I studied those books like manuals. I was more fascinated with the beautiful women and how the pimps got them to do whatever they wanted. I fantasized about having a stable of fabulously exotic women who I would spoil, and they would be loyal to me to the end.

Even back then, I knew I loved beautiful women and wanted to be surrounded by them always. The pimps in the stories always beat their women, but my fantasy was to be "Captain Save a Ho" before I even knew what that was. I guess it was my way of saving my mother from her situation using other beautiful women as substitutes.

* * *

My elementary and middle school years were a blur of trying to do my best in school, keeping up with household chores, taking on the big sister role, and caring for my sister and now brother, and still trying to carve out my own childhood. I had gone from being the only child to now being the stepchild and the eldest with all of the responsibility.

Njoroge adopted me but constantly made it clear that I was not his biological child. He controlled and punished me but denied me any of the fatherly benefits he lavished on my sister and brother. Let me break down the psychological game he hit me with.

First of all, once he became my "father," Njoroge explained to me that whenever he punished me, beat me, it was because he and Mama loved me. He said that if he didn't love me, he would let me just run amok, and he didn't want to do that.

So, I thought that was just what all parents did. Now, I

don't know what offenses warrant a full-fledged beating with my bare ass showing and him using his full-grown man strength to bring down that stinging leather strap, but I got beatings at least 3-5 times weekly. These beatings were sometimes ordered by Mama, to be administered after Njoroge got home from work at 10pm.

These were the worst because I used to feel so utterly betrayed by her. He wasn't my real father, and he would beat her ass, so why the hell did she think he was beating me out of love? I remember the look of disgust he would give Mama sometimes when he first came in the door, and she immediately started ranting about how I was waiting for his beating for some minor thing like talking in class. I felt like she basically handed me over to the abusive predator for his sadistic pleasure.

I had to wait up, scared as shit and preparing my mind for the beating, and then wake up early the next day for school, all whelped up and in pain, and act like nothing ever occurred. So, as my pride grew, I decided that I would not cry because I refused to let Njoroge know that he hurt me, and I wanted to hurt Mama by her knowing she caused this.

Because me not crying was taken as an affront to Njoroge's pride, he would double down with the strap, and Mama would beg me to cry so he would stop. I would take those beatings and go back to my room and sob myself to sleep, sometimes with my sister and brother giggling at me. They never got the same beatings, at least not to the same extent nor for the same minor infractions.

* * *

I really think that this period is what began my struggle with never being or doing enough. This also started my struggle with ego and pride. I came to this earth with a strong sense of pride and independence, so when Njoroge wanted me to show deference to his authority by crying, I just couldn't. I considered crying the weakest thing ever because I always saw my mother crying and begging him to stop beating her. It never worked, so I refused to beg. I would rather he beat me to death than bow down.

The crazy thing about people is that like-minded folks always flock together, be they abusive or abused. Mama's and Njoroge's friends were no different. When we moved to the Bronx, Mama befriended 3 families, the Johnsons, the Browns, and the Williams; out of those, only Mrs. Johnson was not physically abused by her husband.

As a matter of fact, on our 10th floor, there was always some domestic violence shit going on. The lesbian couple next door would always be fighting, and the femme chick would be beaten up in the hallway begging to be let back into her apartment.

My mother would have to routinely run into the stairwell to escape Njoroge's rages and stay there until he passed out drunk. I will never forget the time that Mr. Williams beat the shit out of his wife and put her and all the kids out into the street. I remember looking out of my window and saw them filing out of the building, all carrying plastic bags with their belongings and heading to a shelter. That was one of the saddest things I can remember.

Mrs. Brown finally got sick of her husband's shit, and

she did the Al Green thing on him, except with some hot dog water. I remember silently cheering her on as I ear hustled her, telling Mama how she did it. Mr. Brown used to look like the Mack; he was sharp with the coke pinky nail, the platforms, feathered fedora, and everything. That nigga was never the same after that boiling hot dog water soaked his ass. The last time I saw him, he was all burnt up and living on the park bench down in Harlem close to my school.

* * *

Njoroge's friends were all abusive as well. I figured it was the cultural norm. I still have a big problem with people describing African culture as all Kings and Queens and shea butter.

Every family with a Kenyan male at the head that I encountered growing up was abusive in some way and definitely not empowering for the women. Most of his friends married submissive white women or much younger women that they could control.

One of his friends killed the whole damn family. He pushed the wife out of the 20th floor window, and he jumped with his 2 boys. Years later, another family found out that their husband and father had left a whole family back in Kenya and moved to the United States without telling them.

There was only one family, the Kiaries, who had a wife that wasn't taking her husband's shit. She was a Black American revolutionary sister that would give my mother advice on how to stand up to Njoroge. Still, I guess Mama never had the courage to implement her suggestions.

* * *

Like I said, I was now the eldest child, and I routinely got the speech about helping out as the eldest. So, I used to change diapers, wash the dirty cloth diapers, babysit, clean bathrooms, clean the kitchen, and even cook a little just to ease the load for Mama.

I didn't mind because I figured if I did a good job, I would get some praise from either of them, but it seemed as if it was never, ever good enough no matter what I did. I would consider myself surprising Mama by doing way above and beyond what she asked me to do, things like taking apart the stove and cleaning all the nasty gunk and bugs out till it looked brand new.

Cleaning the bathrooms with all kinds of chemical concoctions I made, almost killing myself mixing those poisons, just so the bathrooms could glisten pristine white like when we first moved in.

I would study and get 95% or even 97%, which was still an A and better than most others in my class. However, it became evident that it was never, ever good enough to get a "good work" or "I'm proud of you" no matter what I did. All I ever got was, "Why didn't you get 100%?" Or Mama would zero in on the one area that I may not have cleaned or picked that one dish that may still have had a little grease on it and go off like I didn't do anything else worthy.

I mean, damn, I was a kid and doing the best I could. I

think they expected perfection, which I came to expect from myself, not knowing this was impossible. This is definitely the root of my issues with harsh self-judgment.

* * *

Njoroge's incessant abuse continued. We couldn't celebrate holidays or go to church. I couldn't straighten my hair because that was trying to be white. We had no friends or family coming to visit because no one fucked with Njoroge.

Mama went from being a slim, fashionable, joyous woman to depressed, 30 pounds heavier, dark circles under her eyes and black and blue marks on her arms from where he would grab her to finally developing gestational diabetes. I would lay awake at night listening to her screams from his drunken punches and rage, terrified that if he beat her to death, I would be left all alone with his ass. We had an outwardly nice, seemingly prosperous life, but it was really hell in that apartment.

All the mothers tried to keep it together for their families and would still plan outings for us on the weekends if just to get out of the oppressive house. I still appreciate that effort because as an adult, I now know that it could have gone another way. The mothers could have given up and sunk into that stagnant depression that abuse brings.

Chapter Four

Summers Abroad

One good thing about being the offspring of immigrants is that you get to travel on a plane to exotic lands and experience adventures that my African American friends didn't get to do.

However, since I was in elementary school, I longed to fit in. I was initially sad that I didn't have any cousins to spend summer "down south" with. I really thought I was missing something by not going down south until I got older and realized going to Kenya or Trinidad for summer vacation was way better than being in the mysterious down south.

I had been going back and forth to Trinidad, unaccompanied sometimes, since I was a toddler, but going to Kenya was a whole other level of adventure. First of all, the speeches from my Mama about female circumcision and getting those damn malaria and yellow fever shots were my least favorite parts of those trips.

Yo! I was seriously horrified when my mother sat me down and told me in hushed tones about how I need to always stick with my female cousins and never wander off alone. She told me how sometimes little girls my age got kidnapped and forcibly circumcised by people in the village because it was their tribal tradition.

I was quite puzzled because, as I said before, I was an avid reader and nosey as shit, so I knew what circumcision was. Also, by the time we visited Kenya, my brother was born, so I knew how painful it was for a baby boy, and I could not imagine why in the hell anyone would want to cut me down there!

This is one of the main reasons that I am not always fond of traditions. Whatever sadistic fuck came up with this way to control women's pleasure is hopefully rotting in hell right now, and shame on the many women who support this fuckery. Now, back to the story…

* * *

We traveled to Kenya, Banana Hill, right outside of Nairobi, to celebrate the birth of my sister and brother and for my mother to meet her new family. I was so surprised to see that his family was pretty decent, especially the women. They were all very welcoming, and the kids, my cousins, all took me under their wings and showed me around the land and farm. It was a far cry from the modern amenities in the Bronx, but it was still modern by Kenyan standards during the 1970s.

Njoroge's father was the head of one of the clans of the Kikuyu tribe. His mother, my Cucu (grandmother), was also well loved in the village. The fact that they owned a lot of land and cattle and had connections to the president Jomo

Kenyatta made the family a big deal in Nairobi.

The wealth was the reason they had a house with indoor plumbing and other Western-style amenities. It is the custom to slaughter and roast different meats when celebrating events like weddings. I believe that our visit was to be a combination wedding reception and a "show off my new family celebration" for Njoroge. It was like in the Bible where the favored son returns home, and they slaughter the fatted calf.

I still love the smell of the wood crackling under the fire and the roasted meat smoke wafting up into the air. It was fascinating to see them skin and drain the animal's blood and use every single part of it for food or clothing. I believe they roasted a cow, a sheep, and a goat. Each meat had its own distinctive taste, and I loved every minute of it on some tribal, carnivorous level.

I think because this is a good memory is the reason why I love grilling to this day. Also, no offense to my Kenyans who can cook, I don't recall the food being particularly seasoned beyond salt.

My experience with Njoroge cooking steaks was that he liked the meat flavor, so he never used seasoning, and his shit was always well done like a leather shoe. I swear I hate steak to this day because of the experience of being forced to eat that nastiness. I like to grill because I guess I have been wanting to perfect the art of grilling some perfectly tender and well-seasoned cuts of meat.

In some way, I feel like this erases the horrible forced eating experiences of my childhood. Kenyans eat a few staple foods like chai tea, chapati bread, mandazi (Kenyan donuts), and samosas. There is a heavy East Indian influence in the foods there because of British colonization, so their food has become a part of the Kenyan culinary identity, similar to Trinidad.

This was also a comfort source because the food was almost like my Granny's, just less spicy. I have always been a natural student of cultures. It was my introduction to how food is one of the equalizers of society. Although I only spoke a little Kikuyu and Swahili, and their English wasn't always the best, I learned a lot more of the language by being taught the various food names.

One of the worst things I ate in Kenya was that nasty-ass hominy. That shit is like cardboard corn on steroids. I still have nightmares that I am choking on those ginormous white kernels, and they keep multiplying in my throat like popcorn choking me!

* * *

So, of course, it wasn't all eating and dancing and shit. We had a couple of incidents that let me know I ain't about that rural life. Them damn insects and animals, what the entire hell!

My poor baby sister got bit half to death by these big red fire ants. My little brother got burned on the little metal camp stove they used to roast corn in. We had to sleep with the mosquito nets enclosing the beds because those jokers were looking like tiny birds.

We went on a safari to some game preserve, and why did the damn baboons jump on the car and start trying to pick the rubber off the back window? They were fucking with us, and I was terrified the whole time in that little-ass car in the middle of lions and elephants, and who knows what other predators were stalking our curious asses?

I prefer to experience my animal encounters at the zoo or on Animal Planet after that safari. I did enjoy exploring the area with my cousins, traipsing through the red clay dirt in my bare feet despite my Mother's warnings about catching a jigger. Of course, because I am hard-headed, I stepped on a jigger and had to get it cut out of my foot.

Jiggers are sand fleas that burrow into your skin and lay eggs if they aren't caught and removed. I learned which plants to avoid and which plants were medicinal and used to soothe the insect bites that became all too common.

* * *

All in all, Kenya was a cool place to visit. I'm looking forward to visiting again as an adult and with a renewed perspective and no longer through the eyes of abuse.

Chapter Five

Big Wanjiku

So, on our first trip to Kenya back in the summer of 1972, upon our return, we brought back Big Wanjiku. She was Njoroge's 17-year-old niece who came to live with us and supposedly to allow her to continue her education and make a better life in the United States.

Big Wanjiku's older sister was supposed to come to America, but she declined because she had become a born again Christian and knew that it would literally be like living in hell coming to another country to live under his roof.

He always was irate about God and refused to hear anything about Christianity. He would argue anyone down that believed in the white Jesus. Njoroge tried to act like he was benevolent by sponsoring his niece to come to the United States, but really he wanted a young servant girl and concubine.

Big Wanjiku came to not offend Njoroge since her sister did not want to go. Njoroge was disgusted that she did not want the opportunity his arrogant ass was supposedly providing her. Wanjiku, being only 17 and naive, jumped at the chance to come to America.

That excitement was short lived, though. Even though she already knew him to be a controlling person, she thought it would still be fine. Apparently, Njoroge was the only boy and doted upon by his mother, so she is the one that created that monster.

* * *

Anyway, while we were in Kenya for about a month, she got her visa together and traveled back home with us. While we were going through Heathrow Airport in London on our transfer, much to everyone's dismay, Njoroge started beating Mama in the public airport because he blamed her for a mistake on the airline tickets, which caused us to have to stay over in London.

We were traveling with my baby sister in her arms, and he still hit her. Njoroge was an insecure, wicked, Godless man. He beat women and children but got beaten up by real men. This was evident when he came back to the house in Kenya after a night out with his friends at the bar all bloodied and beaten. Apparently, he started a fight and got his ass kicked soundly by some real men.

Big Wanjiku knew that was a precursor to the horrific experience she was about to have. She was expecting a Mary Poppins experience but, instead, got Miss Celie in The Color Purple treatment.

Njoroge treated Big Wanjiku like a slave from day one. He took her passport, and when she did get a job, he made her open a joint account with my mother and him, but only he was allowed unrestricted access to the account.

He would constantly threaten her with revoking her visa, like he had that power, to scare her into not leaving. He was always getting drunk and telling her to come to sit on his lap, and he would touch her. When she resisted, he would beat the shit out of her.

She was terrified of him, even to the point of risking her own safety for fear of what he would do to her. I remember an incident with the pressure cooker that, to this day, has me with PTSD.

Since Big Wanjiku was fresh from Kenya, she wasn't familiar with how to fix hot dogs, much less how to use a pressure cooker. She was cooking something and opened the lid without depressurizing it, and it exploded everywhere! Her whole face and arms were burnt, and there was food all over the kitchen, even on the ceiling.

She was so scared of Njoroge that she refused to go to the emergency room before cleaning up the kitchen. Mama knew what was going on with Big Wanjiku and Njoroge, but she was so terrified of her own beatings that she never helped her.

Finally, my Granny came to visit, and she saw her chance to run away from the terror.

Big Wanjiku never wanted to leave us kids in the house because we were all young. I was around 7, and my siblings were 2 and 1. She basically sacrificed her safety to care for us until Granny came to relieve her.

One night, Njoroge beat her so badly she decided to make a run for it. Big Wanjiku ran upstairs to the neighbor, Ms. Brown, the only one who stood up to her own alcoholic, abusive husband. She hid her overnight in the apartment.

When Njoroge came looking for her, Ms. Brown told him if he tried to come to her house, it would be the last thing he ever did. That punk ass backed down, and the next day Big Wanjiku was able to escape to her friend's apartment in Queens, where she stayed for years.

* * *

This asshole apparently tracked her down and went to her job and tried to beat and kidnap her to come back to the Bronx. This was after she turned 18 and was of legal age! Luckily the police intervened, and she was able to get away.

I never knew whatever happened to her because no one ever spoke about her again. Njoroge wrote a letter to her parents telling them that she became a prostitute, not knowing that she had already traveled back to Kenya and given them the whole story.

Years later, when my mother was celebrating her second wedding at Sylvia's in Harlem, she was reunited with Big Wanjiku, who had been thriving as a waitress there for many years. I was so happy to learn that she turned out quite all right despite those horrific experiences at the hand of that asshole, Njoroge.

Chapter Six

Music and Good Times

As I said before, I spent a great deal of my childhood immersed in books, music, and television. These things allowed me to dissolve into another world and temporarily forget the tensions in my own house.

Television time was one of the few halfway peaceful times because there was no conversation. It was the 70s, and the burgeoning era of Black sitcoms and pretty bad-ass women, and I was about it all!

We would all sit down in the living room after dinner and watch Good Times, Maude, All in the Family, and the favorite was The Jeffersons. We all loved seeing a whole Black family winning and being able to talk to White people any kind of way with no consequences. That wasn't the case on TV until the Jeffersons moved on up.

* * *

Back in 1977, when I was about 10 years old and in the 7th grade, the mini-series Roots came out, and that set some shit off in NYC! For the next week in school, it was tense as hell between the mostly Black and Brown students and the White teachers.

The air was thick as peanut butter with the rage of every Black person in America and the discomfort and shame of White people. Even Ronald Reagan just had to weigh in saying, "I don't know how anyone can stay home for 8 days straight to watch the series." Trying to throw shade because the ratings showed that everyone of all races was tuned in to view the African-American experience.

* * *

Around the same time, I began to figure out I really liked pretty women, preferably brunettes. I didn't discriminate in my daydreams. I liked Lola Falana, Jayne Kennedy, Maria from Sesame Street, and every single Catwoman, and I loved me some Cher.

Then I discovered my first crushes, Charlie's Angels, Wonder Woman, and Days of Our Lives' Deidre Hall. I used to have their posters hidden under my bed cause Mama and Njoroge didn't allow any White women on the wall. I would take them out on Saturday nights and perform to them while listening to the disco radio station.

I would imagine myself wining and dining them, showering them with tennis bracelets and sexy tennis outfits to go with it. In my mind, I was already suave as shit! I couldn't wait to grow up and start meeting beautiful women.

I was so obsessed with Charlie's Angels that when NYC had the blackout of July 1977, I cried because Charlie's Angels were supposed to come on that night. I also cried because I wished I could have been out there looting with the rest of the city. In my mind, that was the perfect opportunity for a fashion come up.

That get-over spirit was deep in me by then. I had started shoplifting already, stealing magazines and little trinkets to bribe my little snitch sister. I had to take inconspicuous things that my mother couldn't find. Things small enough that she would believe that I could buy with my bullshit $5 allowance for cleaning the house like a professional maid service. I figured out quickly that taking cash was the best; this way, I could ball out at the candy truck and play grown with my friends.

I was resentful of Mama and Njoroge's treatment of me, so I believe that's what gave me the idea to just take what I want. I learned from their behavior that no matter how well I did in school, how immaculately I cleaned the house, how carefully I looked after my siblings, I was never going to get anything I wanted unless I got it for myself.

* * *

Njoroge was always a bit of a hustler and a shrewd businessman, so sometime in the late 70s, he started selling African artifacts at various street festivals and the Bleecker Street Flea Market. Much to Mama's dismay, he forced her to help him with all the physical labor of setting up and tearing down the display tables.

After working all week, he still expected her to be fully involved in his vending business. However, she never got a dime for her troubles.

I always looked forward to going to these festivals because I realized the potential for cash money and the opportunity to meet many interesting people. I found that I actually loved being a salesperson – I had the gift of gab, and it brought me money!

I mean, I had to steal it from him, but I got it. It made me feel worthy like I could finally do something I wanted for myself with my own cash.

I started stealing from Njoroge's wallet around middle school age; I believe I was about 9 years old. Around the same time I discovered Newports, Olde English and Pink Champale. Let me explain. So, we used to go on end of year field trips to amusement parks like Great Adventure in New Jersey or Rye Playland in Rye, NY, and, of course, we needed money for the rides and food. After seeing Njoroge count out stacks of money he made over the weekend, he would grudgingly dole out $5 for me to take on the trip. $5 doesn't buy shit in NY now, and it didn't back then either. So, I was like, OK I'm about to get mine. I would wait until he went into the shower, and I would slip a large bill like a $50 or $100 out of his wallet. I took large bills because he didn't think that I would be bold enough to steal that much or even be able to spend it because I was so young. Little did he know about the candy truck and the bodegas. As long as you have cash in New York, no one bats an eye. This was way before the age restrictions on tobacco and liquor. I always thought the ladies in the cigarette ads were sexy, and I wanted to try my hand at looking grown, so I picked up smoking. I would always say that I was getting the cigarettes and liquor for my

Mama and this was the only denomination she had. This way I could break the large bills without suspicion. My most memorable trip was to Rye Playland because my friends and I got drunk off Pink Champale outside on the bench before heading to the chartered bus. I treated everyone to rides and candy because I couldn't return home with any money. Both he and Mama suspected me after a while, but they could never prove it, so I got away with it.

Chapter Seven

I Couldn't Take It Anymore!

So, for my whole elementary school period, I basically got a beating at least twice weekly for some infraction, real or perceived, and Njoroge's abusive treatment had me thinking that I was a horrible, misbehaved child. I was so shocked when at my 4th-grade graduation, I kept getting called up for every single award that the school gave out. Until then, I had no idea that I was a good student!

One day, Mama was crying after an argument or something, and I had this dreadful feeling that Njoroge would beat her to death after a while. I decided at that time that I was going to kill myself. After all, I couldn't bear the thought of living with Njoroge without Mama because I knew he didn't want me. I didn't really want to do anything painful, so I took like 3 adult aspirin and basically thought I would lay down to sleep and die peacefully.

Not long after I took the aspirin, I wrote a little suicide note, "Goodbye Mama. I have to go now because nodoby loves me." I started getting scared because I realized I may have made a mistake. I didn't really want to die yet. I told

Mama what I did, and she straight up laughed at me and called me stupid because I spelled nobody wrong!

I was hysterical, and she told me that I was dramatic and she was going to be fine. I couldn't believe that she really showed no compassion because I felt that much despair at that age. I was 7 years old. After that incident, I started wishing death upon her, too.

I was like fuck everybody. I kept all my feelings to myself. The outcome I expected was what I saw on TV in the 30-minute sitcoms; at the end, parents and children hug it out and reaffirm their love for each other. I should have known better, but believe me, I learned my lesson that day.

* * *

Despite Mama's constant betrayal of me, I still considered myself her protector. Even Granny, who Mama definitely did not get along with, stepped up to protect Mama from Njoroge because she seemingly was too scared to stand up for herself.

I remember once when Granny came up from Trinidad to meet her new grandchildren. I was so proud when she confronted Njoroge as he was about to hit Mama. Granny was like, "The audacity and disrespect of this Nigga!" She said, "My daughter may be foolish enough to take this treatment from you, but you will NOT hit her in my presence!"

Granny picked up the glass milk jug that we used to get delivered and threatened to smash it over his head. I came and stood next to her like, "If you hit my Granny, Nigga you are dying today." Njoroge turned and walked away like the punk ass he was. I knew that I came from true warrior stock that day.

* * *

So, after our Kenyan trip, Njoroge brought back some beautiful artifacts, including a gorgeous carved ebony walking stick and a handmade, beaded designed wooden stool, which he kept in the master bedroom.

One night, as I lay awake seething with anger listening to Mama scream and beg Njoroge to leave her alone, I jumped up and couldn't take it any fucking more. I remember bursting through the door and striding into their bedroom with murderous intent.

Njoroge was naked and standing on the side of the bed, trying to rape Mama. It was rape because she clearly did not want to be with him. Njoroge immediately went into charm mode and put on this grin. He said, "Wanjiru, Hi, what are you doing here? Go back to bed. This is between me and your mother."

Mama was sitting up in the bed with the sheets pulled up over her chest, trying to keep her dignity. I just kept on walking towards the bed and looking to see what I could hit Njoroge with. I looked to my left and saw the walking stick; I tried to lift it, but it was too heavy for me.

Right next to it was the little wooden stool, and that was the perfect weight for me to hoist. I picked that stool up, stepped up onto the bed, and stepped over Mama while she was screaming for me to go back to bed.

By this time, Njoroge had crouched down beside the bed, so I could not see his nakedness. All the time, he kept saying, "Wanjiru, what are you doing? Go back to bed!"

All I saw was red. I took that stool by the legs and turned it upside down, and bashed Njoroge on the head with the flat part. BAM! That motherfucker passed out. Mama screamed and said, "Oh My God, you killed him!" I turned and looked at her so evil I felt the murderous rage and disgust well up in me. I said very calmly, "Good." And stared at her for a few seconds.

I will never forget the fear in her eyes when she realized that I really meant to kill him. I was so mad at her because I was trying to protect her, and now she was scared of me?! That night, I jumped down off the bed and went back to my room and had the most peaceful sleep I ever had since Njoroge came into my life.

The next morning, when he woke up, Njoroge called me over and said, "So I heard you tried to kill me last night?" I said, very calmly, "I did and if you ever touch my mother again, I will kill you."

He just looked at me. I guess he took me seriously because he bought me a bike, and the beatings slacked up a bit. I guess he and Mama didn't know if I was for real a psychopath or just had mega balls to confront him.

They were a bit shook. I actually never got a full-fledged beating again until the incident—the incident which I never wanted to name and have never written a word about until now.

The incident so traumatized me that I blocked out a

whole year and a half of my life.

My anger was clearly deepening because I really found my voice in middle school. Usually, I was content to blend into the crowd and not be seen. I had stopped raising my hand and participating in class for fear of being wrong and embarrassing myself. Also, again trying to blend in and not be seen as too smart by my peers. Anyway, when I was in about the 5th grade, I got suspended for fighting and cursing this boy out after he said something about my Mama. I was terrified because I knew I was going to get the serious beatdown once she and Njoroge found out. I was pleasantly surprised when they gave me a talking to instead and explained while stifling laughter that somebody saying, "Your Mama," wasn't anything I should jeopardize my school record over. She said, "I don't know that boy and you don't have to defend me." She gave me the whole sticks and stones speech and how words don't harm me, so I should ignore these taunts in the future. However, the lesson I learned from that experience was that violence and cursing gets you respect. The fact that I bucked up against a boy and got suspended for some reason gave me some clout. When I came back to school, kids that never spoke to me before were telling me how they were impressed with my cussing finesse. I gained an in with the kids not in the advanced classes with me, and it felt good not to just be the smart kid. I also realized that if I let my temper out, it could get out of control very quickly. I can go from 0 to 100, real quick. I surprised myself with how much rage I released on that boy with no fear of getting my ass kicked. I literally saw red.

Chapter Eight

Supernatural Experiences

I was always a voracious reader, and my favorite subjects were the Black or immigrant experiences and the supernatural. Anything about mythology, fairy tales, and the spirit world was intriguing to me. I was drawn to all of it.

I would seek out stories from other cultures and marvel at the similarities of the stories' morals. This was what got me to expand my view of religion and spiritual things at that early age. I don't know if it was because I was reading about it, but I started to notice strange things happening around me.

Things like, I would place an item down, and then it would disappear. I could look all over, and then when I talked to it out loud, it would miraculously reappear! Things like that I could tolerate because they were mainly mischievous like a child.

* * *

I remember one of my earliest supernatural experiences, which truthfully is like a mist in my memory, but I remember the feelings of fear vividly, then complete peace as it happened.

I was out at Nassau Beach with Mama and some of her friends, my Godparents. As always, I was buried in a book and not paying attention to my surroundings. I was playing on one of those wooden docks looking at things that are found on the beach. I don't know how to swim, but my mother thought it was safe because I was stationary.

However, I remember looking up a while later, and I was slowly drifting further out from the shore. I looked back to the beach, and Mama and her friends were frantically screaming and waving at me to come back.

I was terrified because I had no idea how I even got out there that far. I remember looking out at the vast body of water and feeling so incredibly helpless. A numbing fear spread from my stomach to my heart. I was stuck.

Suddenly, I was no longer scared, and I felt the dock being pushed towards the beach. No one swam out to get me, no lifeguards, nothing visible was in that water with me.

I believe that was the very first time I experienced my guardian angel, to my knowledge. Once I got back to the shore, Mama, with tears in her eyes, hugged me with relief, and my Godparents, whom I never saw again, were asking me what happened.

Of course, being so young, around 4 years old, I couldn't articulate those feelings of fear then peace, but I never forgot that incident. Mama and I never really talked about what happened after that.

Many of my stories that I remember so vividly she claims never happened, but I don't care. I know exactly what happened, and I have never been in denial about things logic cannot explain. Nothing is coincidental in this life, no brief encounter, no event or life choice, nothing. Everything works together for God's purpose at some point in our lives.

* * *

The next experience I remember still profoundly sticks out in my mind. I was running home from elementary school one afternoon, and there was a thunderstorm. I remembered how my Granny always told me to stay away from trees during a thunderstorm because I may be struck by lightning.

Unfortunately, the block that I was running down was tree-lined, and I couldn't really avoid them. As I was running, just as my right foot was in midair getting ready to run directly under a tree, I felt an invisible hand push my chest back, so I couldn't take that step. Right then, a bolt of lightning struck the ground in front of me. I remember thinking, the devil is trying to kill me early, and I silently thanked the unseen force and ran home. I couldn't wait to tell my Granny what happened.

* * *

However, I distinctly remember one incident that was a bit more sinister; it happened to occur when I read The Amityville Horror story. I was sitting in the living room on the couch, and Mama and Njoroge were in the kitchen, and my brother and sister were running around the room playing.

I was totally immersed in my book, reading with my brand new glasses that I just got that day. Suddenly, the room got still, and I felt like I was in a bubble, and I was the only one in the room. This little pebble appeared out of nowhere on the floor a few feet away from the couch. I was mesmerized by this pebble, and it began to roll slowly towards me.

I couldn't move; I couldn't speak. I was just entranced by the pebble, and when it got right in front of my feet, it suddenly flew at me and hit me right in the bridge of my glasses, and they broke in two!

Only then was I able to let out a shriek, and Mama came running out of the kitchen to see my glasses on the floor. Of course, she was furious and even more so when she heard my explanation of what really happened. She accused me of lying and made me tape up my glasses and wear them until we could get back to get another pair, which I assumed would be never.

You know I got a beating for that one. I don't know if I tapped into something in that book, but I know that shit freaked me out. From that day on to now, I have slept with the lights on…even though that shit happened in broad daylight.

As much as I loved horror movies and Stephen King, I slowed up on those after that experience. I remember borrowing the book The Exorcist from the library. I couldn't even get past the first chapter because I knew this was a true story, and I sure didn't want to tap into anything in that book.

I also used to have dreams where something kept me from breathing or moving, sleep paralysis, and I learned to scream out for Jesus in my mind. Instantly, the presence went away. I also used to have such vivid dreams of flying and jumping in the clouds, and right before I woke up,

I could feel my body land with a thump. All these experiences caused me to do a lot of research on the supernatural as I got older. That was when I learned all the terms for my experiences, like astral projection and sleep paralysis. All my life, I have felt like God was allowing me to experience these things in preparation for my later mission in life, whatever that was going to be. I knew it would include some type of spiritual teachings. Not that I wanted any of that.

* * *

I'm not sure that I had these experiences because I drew them to myself because of my interest in the supernatural power. I guess I used to like horror movies for the same reason – it was thrilling but not likely to happen to me, so I could deal with it. After I learned a bit more over the years about the true power of spirits and demons, I stayed far away from any form of it. Unfortunately, that wasn't until well into my 30s.

I loved flirting with danger. I think my interest in the supernatural came from the desire for power over my circumstances in life. For instance, while we still lived with Njoroge, I was obsessed with learning different ways to kill someone stealthily.

Growing up in NYC, the concrete jungle, I was taught to be alert to my surroundings at all times and always look out for danger. Basically, I was obsessed with trying not to become a victim, so I would imagine all the ways I would defend myself if a situation presented itself. I would imagine me gouging out eyes with my keys, biting noses off, shooting people with a gun armed with a silencer through the pocket of my coat.

My logic was that I wanted to let the offender know that they fucked with the wrong kid, but I never wanted to stick around for the cops to come. Anyway, after reading about witchcraft and spells, I figured this was an even better way to control people and my circumstances in stealth mode. I was hooked.

Chapter Nine

13. I was 13 Motherfucker.

So, Mama got pregnant with my youngest brother AJ in late 1979. Because of the stress of her home life and gestational diabetes, she was hospitalized for the last couple of months of her pregnancy.

That left me home with Njoroge and my siblings. This motherfucker must have been just waiting for the chance to get me alone. Apparently, he had already tried to rape his niece who lived with us briefly, which is why she ran away. We never found this out until about 20 years later, but that is another part of the story...

By this time, I had gotten into one of the most prestigious schools in NY, Bronx High School of Science, and I was in my freshman year. I had already started cutting up and hanging out instead of going to class, so I guess my grades started slipping.

One spring evening, after my brother and sister were put to bed, my mother was in the hospital. Njoroge was home drinking his Johnny Walker Red; he decided to "discipline" me because of my grades.

This started out with him coming after me with a metal broomstick, and I was deflecting those blows like Wonder Woman. I had welts and was bleeding a little on my forearms from blocking the broom, but I kept fighting.

Finally, he said, "I don't believe you are a virgin. I think you have been fucking around, and I need to make sure you're still a virgin. Get in the bedroom!"

I was so shocked that I didn't know what to say. I finally started begging him to not do this. I was a virgin, and I had plans for my virginity, not plans to lose it with his nasty ass.

He kept telling me to be quiet, so I didn't wake my siblings. He wrestled me to the bed and pulled my pants and panties off; even drunk, he was much stronger than me, of course, so finally, I had to just lay there and take it.

He stuck his index finger in me roughly and kept saying, "It's not tight enough; you are not a virgin." Finally, he got his pants down and rammed his penis into me; I felt the pain and the blood and then the disgusting semen running down my thighs.

I went numb right then and there. I think I kind of left my body because I was so ultimately humiliated and felt absolutely defiled. I have the spirit of a warrior, and I felt like he broke me right then.

After he finished, he pulled his pants up and told me I better not tell anyone, or he would kill me. He kept saying that he would kill me and no one would believe me anyway if I told anyone—all the time in my mind, I was plotting how to get away from him that next morning.

I had to make him think that I was too scared to tell, so I went and took a shower, washed all the semen off of me, and acted like I was scared of him. My main thing was making him believe I was going to school as normal. I knew in my heart that if I didn't get away then, it would happen again, and I would definitely end up dead.

That next morning, he kept reiterating the death threats, and I kept saying, "Yes, I understand." As soon as Njoroge went back upstairs to the apartment, I ran back into the building and went to our neighbor, Mrs. Johnson.

Her husband was a cop, and her brother was a gangster,

so I felt like they would be my protectors. Thank God I was correct. They called the police. Once they got there, Mrs. Johnson and her brother escorted me terrified back up to the apartment to arrest Njoroge.

This Nigga acted like he had no idea what was going on. While he was arguing with the police, Mama happened to call the house, and he ran and grabbed the phone before I could get to it. We weren't going to tell my mother what happened until he was actually in jail because she was already under such stress. We didn't want to jeopardize the baby.

However, this Nigga set everything in motion by grabbing the phone. He was arrested and placed in the Tombs, the Bronx jail, where Mrs. Johnson's gangster brother arranged to get his ass kicked.

That day the course of my life changed forever, and here it is, almost 40 years later, I am still dealing with the ramifications of that incident. Even after he has been dead for almost a decade, the emotional remnants of that sordid act still haunt me.

I will never regret my actions in reporting him and taking the chance of my reputation being dragged through the courts. I know that my act of courage broke the cycle of abuse for my whole family, and I could not have lived with myself one more day if I did nothing. Now, this is where my life began again....

Post Rape...

* * *

POST RAPE EMOTIONS

SHOCK

DENIAL

NUMB

DISGUST

RAGE

REVENGE

REASSURANCE

SADNESS

REPLAY

SELF LOATHING

ANGRY AT MYSELF

GUILT

BURIAL

COLDNESS

DETERMINATION

ERASURE OF ALL EMOTIONS

BITTER BITCH INSIDE

CHAMELEON/ PEOPLE PLEASER OUTSIDE

* * *

So, after Njoroge rolled his disgusting drunk, sweaty ass off of me, I felt like I had an out-of-body experience. I was completely in shock that the act that I had read about in so many books before had actually happened to me.

When I read about it, I wondered how the women survived the physical act of degradation and brutality. I never knew about the lifelong emotional toll that rape takes on victims.

My first thought was if sex feels like this, then I don't know what the hype is about because that shit hurt like hell. I was also so sad that my virginity was lost to this asshole.

I was taught that your virginity was like a prize you held on to for your loved person. I wasn't even sure that I wanted a man, but I at least thought I would have had the choice of who I gave it up to.

* * *

I also kept asking myself if I felt any different since the rape. I remember feeling embarrassed explaining to teachers, lawyers, police, and my friends what happened. This was my first time ever dealing with the justice system, and I felt once again thoroughly violated by this tedious and traumatic process.

I had to keep explaining in explicit detail the timeline of events. In my embarrassment, I worked hard to appear emotionless; I never wanted to show that Njoroge affected me in any way. My welts on my arms and knuckles were scabbed over, but I minimized the amount of pain I was in.

My warrior spirit and pride kicked into overdrive, and I

basically withdrew into a silent building rage. Every time I had to say the words "my vagina" and "his penis," I became more disgusted and angry with myself that I didn't see this coming, that I didn't fight harder, that I didn't kill him earlier, that I didn't go live with my Granny in Trinidad.

I had to testify in front of the grand jury, so Njoroge could be indicted. The worst thing about the court proceedings was that after reliving that trauma in detail out loud in front of strangers and Njoroge, my abuser, my testimony was inadmissible in court because of my age. WTF!!!!!

When I found that out, I was outraged. I decided that the Injustice system doesn't work for the victims, especially rape victims. I'll never forget the way my heart dropped to my stomach when I learned he had gotten off.

I had come back to the apartment to get some clothes since I stayed with Aunt Isabel in Manhattan, and I answered the phone. Njoroge was on the other end, and he said, with a chilling tone, "I was acquitted. Do you know what that word means?" I said, "I guess it means the opposite of convicted because you're not calling collect."

He said, "That's right and remember what I said I was going to do to you if you told anyone?" I said, "Yep," and hung up the phone. Apparently, the fact that I had cut class showed that I was a liar and couldn't tell the truth about being raped. Also, washing away the evidence didn't help me either.

My next move was to get revenge because I knew that I couldn't get justice from the system. I had a friend in 9th grade, Juliet, and she had some connections to get a gun, so I asked her to bring me one to school. I told her what had happened to me, and she agreed to get me a gun to handle my business.

I guess God intervened at the time because she did come with the gun and her older brother. He explained that he could give me the gun and I could kill Njoroge, but I would go to jail, and my consequences for that would be greater than the rape violation. He talked some sense into me, and I decided to deal with it another way, by ignoring it.

I decided that I was going to put it behind me and that I was all right. My physical wounds would heal, and I could get back to normal. Although my life was completely shattered, we had to move. I changed schools and lost all my friends; the family was separated, and we were broke.

* * *

The incident took place the last week of May 1980, so I still had to finish my last 2 months of 9th grade. I was so blown that we had to move because that meant I was no longer eligible to go to the best high school in New York, Bronx High School of Science.

Only the elite students were admitted to the school, and I was one of the minority of the minorities; it hurt to give up that coveted spot. School was the place where I excelled effortlessly, and if I was no longer a part of the "smart crowd," I lost a bit of my direction and identity.

I guess I liked feeling a bit special and belonging to the smart crowd; up to that point, that was a great part of my self-esteem. The rare times I received any praise was in regard to how smart I was. I felt like now even that good thing was gone.

This was also the year I got introduced by Ann Marie to my best friend, Mary Jane, on the bus home after school. In New York, any bus or train primarily used by high school students reeked of that good cheeba cheeba, and the bus drivers never said a word.

By then, I was into pretty brunettes, and Ann Marie was a raven-haired, petite bronze-skinned Italian girl. She was a senior and had a punk vibe going on with the perfectly feathered hair. She pulled out a fat j and lit it up, then passed it to me, and I played it off like I did that shit all the time.

Until that smoke hit the back of my throat, and I coughed up a lung. She laughed her ass off, but after that initial burn went away, I was hooked! I felt like I was walking on air, and I wanted that shit to last forever. It got to the point where I pretty much stopped going to all my classes except English, and I stayed high all the time in the park across from the school with the White boys.

I was so depressed that I would stay out with my friends after school as long as possible before taking that long train ride to Central Park West. I stayed with Aunt Isabel in Manhattan. My brother and sister were staying with my newly discovered mother's half-sister, Auntie Dorothy.

Auntie Dorothy was an abusive color struck bitch, and I felt so bad for my siblings because she treated them like dogs. She literally made them stay out in the hot-ass yard with the dogs all day. Although I was staying in luxury and had everything I wanted, it felt so empty without my family. I used to walk around with my Sony Walkman and big headphones on with the music loud to drown out my sad thoughts. To this day, some songs bring me to tears because I would hear them during that period. I couldn't listen to "Lover's Holiday" by Luther until recently because the trigger was so deep.

* * *

Once my brother was born and Mama was released from the hospital, we would have to find somewhere else to live, especially since Njoroge was not going to be in prison. This was when God showed us favor and showed up miraculously in the form of Ms. Eleanor Perser.

Since I was so young when this happened, I had no idea about the logistics or money it would take to uproot our lives and move somewhere affordable and safe in New York City. I remember talking to Mama and trying to offer my little savings bonds and babysitting money as if that would help in some way to ease the financial burden.

She was terrified and totally clueless as to what was going to happen to our family. So, apparently, while she was recovering in Jacobi Hospital in the Bronx, one of her nurses happened to be Ms. Perser, who took Mama under her wing and proceeded to show her how to navigate life as a single mother.

She showed Mama how to get on the social service system to get some food and WIC assistance, despite her fierce pride and resistance to do so. We ended up moving to Yonkers, the next city above the Bronx in Westchester county. Apparently, the apartments were more affordable there, probably because they were old-ass tenement buildings.

Still, it sufficed in our time of crisis. Mama was quite naïve and honest to a fault, so Mrs. Perser basically put her on to get as much public assistance as possible because of the size of our family and her now single income. She turned us on to various public programs like after school programs and free lunch programs.

Of course, I took it to the next level by ensuring I hit up every free government food handout I could get on the bus. Since I was the primary cook in the house, I had to make sure we always had the good government cheese because we ate a lot of grilled cheese, cereal with the powdered milk, and that nasty peanut butter you had to mix up before making a sandwich.

We were on some straight-up struggle shit, sleeping on mattresses that we got from the second-hand store and furniture from people's trash that Ms. Perser's garbage man boyfriend would bring us from his route.

Our apartment was a second-floor walk-up, complete with mice and roaches that acted like they paid rent. To this day, I am scared to look in the drawer under the stove. I got fucking PTSD from the damn mice! I remember my disgust as I was cleaning out the coat closet, trying to find the source of a disgusting rotting smell. To my horror, I stepped on the crunchy skeleton of a dead mouse. Thank God I am neurotic about wearing slippers because I know I would have tried to amputate my foot if I had touched that shit with my bare skin.

* * *

One other source of poverty PTSD was the creepy, nasty-ass perverted building superintendent. The laundry room was in the damp and dark basement of the building. For some reason, every time I went down there, the fucking super would come up behind me, acting like he didn't have any other place to walk, rubbing his little dick on me.

I was so disgusted, but I never said anything because I didn't want to make any more trouble for Mama. The super was the one who allowed her to have the apartment at a reduced rate, so I figured I had to take one for the team.

By this time, I figured out that justice was nonexistent, so I needed to handle this independently. When I got grown and had my own apartment, one of my earliest standards was that I needed the washer and dryer in my apartment or at least on my floor. I needed to make a quick getaway if anyone tried to violate me in the laundry room.

While writing this, I am truly discovering how so many of my decisions are based upon traumatic experiences. We started to settle into our new lives in Yonkers, and life seemed to get back to normal.

Chapter Ten

Moving to "The Country", Yonkers

So, I was already mad that I had to leave my elite high school in the Bronx and had to move to the country, at least in my eyes. I wasn't trying to go to the new school because I assumed that everyone was slow and country.

I considered myself a sophisticated New Yorker. Yep, at 13 I just knew I was the shit, and everyone I met had never left Yonkers! I was so blown because I had been traveling the subways all across the city for my whole life, and it wasn't even like Manhattan was that far from Yonkers. However, the pace wasn't lightning fast as the City, and I hated it. I cracked up when I met other teens that thought they were hard, and they had no clue what hard was. During this period is when I learned quite a few lessons about life by sheer observation.

The first lesson I learned was that being rebellious and underperforming in school would only hurt me in the end. Mama started going to Messiah Baptist Church. There was a presentation by one of the vice principals, Mrs. Muriel King, and she was a take-no-shit kind of person.

I had started acting out by not listening and staying out past my curfew. Mama thought I needed some supervision while at school. Back then, it was definitely a network of caretakers, the proverbial village, that got you successfully through school. This was also Mama's way of steering me towards a different way of life than the one I was headed to.

Since I felt derailed in life, I had started to not give a fuck about school, which would be my only way out of a dead-end life. Ms. Muriel gave me an after school job in her office doing some administrative stuff since I had already learned to type fluently. She also ensured I was assigned to all the advanced academic classes the school offered and made me bring her my grades regularly to make sure I wasn't bullshitting.

She and my mother were dead-ass that I better not get anything less than an 'A' because I was more than capable of doing the work. Anything less was sheer laziness.

Ms. Muriel also assigned me to the Black guidance counselor, Mr. Eddie Ferrell, who turned out to be DJ Eddie F's father. He was so damn cool, and I think I tried to imitate a bit of his swagger.

I was impressed to see a sharp-dressed, intelligent Black man. He always kept it casual and relatable when it came to advice. Between both of them, they convinced me that succeeding in academia was the way to go if I didn't want to grow up making minimum wage and being miserable.

* * *

Right around 1979, my freshman year in high school at Bronx Science, hip-hop culture and rap music started to blow up. Growing up in the Bronx, I was very familiar with the park jams the local DJs used to throw. The park across the street from my apartment building was always jumping.

The DJs would set up the enormous speakers and turntables in the handball court and rock until late into the evening. I would be damn near about to fall out of the window trying to listen to the thumping bass long after I was supposed to be in bed asleep.

I remember being in art class one afternoon, and suddenly, over the school loudspeaker, someone started blaring "Rapper's Delight." The only other Black guy in the class and I nearly lost our minds! That one rebellious act of taking over the school mic and playing SugarHill Gang probably cemented my hip hop fanatic status to this day.

After that, I was obsessed with hip hop, breakdancing, and graffiti; the whole culture was my shit! I was basically this skinny, smart, nerdy girl who read incessantly, but secretly, I admired the whole swag of street culture.

Hip hop music gave me a chance to express and develop my swag. That combination of confidence and rage that was building inside me was right at home in the braggadocio lyrics of Melle Mel, Kurtis Blow, SugarHill, Jimmy Spicer aka Superrhymes, Spoonie Gee, Sequence, and the greatest DJ of all time Grandmaster Flash and the Furious 5.

I was never allowed to go to party at places like the infamous Disco Fever, so the radio and my small wax collection was what I had. I wanted to rock the Pumas, Kangols, Adidas tracksuits and shell toes that all the Bboys rocked, but of course, the way Mama's money was set up, that wasn't happening for me. I had to sing along to the music and imagine, which I did well. Being in New York, though, allowed me to get some good bootleg stuff, so I was still styling, kinda.

* * *

Once I moved to Yonkers, they got the culture a little slower, so all I had was the radio to hear my beloved rap music. We had one little record store at the bottom of Locust Hill, my old street, and they used to get all my little after school job money once they started carrying rap albums. I would stop in there as much as possible on my trips to Getty Square to run errands for Mama because they would be blasting music outside to entice customers to buy the new releases. Also, hip hop had minimal airplay back then, so the Mom and Pop record stores were the ones who really popularized the music by playing and selling it.

My 10th grade year in 1980 – I was about 15 – was when I started setting these lofty goals for myself, basically to impress my Mama and other adults who kept telling me I was so smart and had such potential. According to them, I was going places, and I started to buy into the hype although I really had no idea what I wanted to do.

I won an essay contest and in writing my bio for the newspaper I had to come up with something impressive about my goals after receiving this honor. So, I started saying I wanted to be a lawyer and, eventually, the first Black woman Supreme Court Justice. I had no clue how lofty an undertaking this was, but it sounded ambitious, so I went with it.

Mama believed the idle hands are the devil's playground thing, so she always kept us in some after school program. We also got involved in the National Council of Negro Women, the NAACP, and the church activities. My life was taken up by things others decided, so I rebelled by doing things I wanted to do, and I was as stubborn as hell.

* * *

My high school years were my first time taking in life lessons about working, sex, men, addiction, religion, and classism in the African-American community. I learned quickly that I had an addictive personality. Once I liked something, I became obsessed and had to have it daily until I got physically sick of it.

I know my lunch for at least one whole school year was a meatball hero with extra cheese, Entenmann's crumb cake, and a quart of Tropicana orange juice. I felt the same way when I was introduced to porn; I was hooked!

Back then, 42nd Street in NYC was a seedy place with porn theaters and peep shows on every block. An HBO show now called The Deuce represents the Times Square I grew up with.

I had first seen porn newspapers under the mattress when we lived with Njoroge, so my appetite was already whetted by those. But, I figured out I could cut school and sneak into the adult movies and watch to my heart's content as long as I could get past the ticket taker.

So, I would dress up like a man, complete with a hat or hoodie, pay for my ticket and make sure I sat in a row by myself and was fascinated by all the freaky tricks and fetishes performed by Seka and Vanessa Del Rio. Once the theater manager found out I was a girl, he would try to come to sit next to me and ask me to compare his shriveled up dick to the ones on the screen.

I know I hurt his ego because I laughed in his face, but he was happy to have someone see his dick. I know he hadn't got any in a while; he was an unfortunate-looking motherfucker. I contemplated getting money from him and other horny dudes in the theater because I knew they would pay, but after one time, I was too disgusted to do it again.

After I found out about S&M and dominatrixes, I wished I could have done that. I could beat a man's ass and stomp on his dick and get paid. What's not to love about that?

After a couple of theater managers and movie watchers figured out I was a girl, the jig was up. I could no longer go to the movies on 40 Deuce incognito, so I indulged my porn addiction with erotica and magazines. I figured out that my vivid imagination worked well enough to make me orgasm without any physical touch.

Those stories of the delivery man coming to drop off some dick came alive in my mind like a 3D movie. I liked the erotic books even more than the movies because I could imagine exotic-looking people, unlike the average white people in real porn.

I wasted most of that school year cutting class to stay home becoming intimately acquainted with myself and fantasize until I moved on to the next obsession, The Club.

* * *

Another lesson I learned was basically to keep my head on a swivel when dealing with men, especially the ones my mother chose because she was so damn naïve.

It always baffled me that she would seemingly settle for these dudes that were clearly not in her intelligence or ambition league, definitely not looks! She met this creepy Jamaican dude, Errol, and I was so mad at her that she basically let this Nigga move in for a minute into our new Yonkers apartment.

I mean, we had just rid ourselves of a predator Nigga, and she let this fool come into our space willingly?! WTF?

So, old school rules stated that you had to be respectful to your elders, and since this Nigga was my elder, although I didn't trust him and I vocalized this, I still had to be polite to him.

I think he was around because he worked on the car or something. Still, I distinctly remember him wanting to drive me to school, and I resisted until Mama told me I was rude, and I got into the car with him grinning like a fox and shit. I was so close to the passenger door that I was damn near outside. When we got to the school, he leaned over for a kiss goodbye, and I was disgusted and scrambled out of the car before he could really get to me.

He was all dusty in his drywall hanging overalls. He had nasty-ass fingernails and scruffy patches of facial hair, and I wasn't trying to be in the same space with him ever.

I told Mama about him trying to kiss me, and she said, "Aw he didn't mean anything by it." Again, WTF.

I never got in the car with him again after that. I insisted upon walking to school with my friends living on Locust Hill.

Shortly afterward, my Granny came to visit, and again she was my saving grace. She chastised Mama for having this Nigga around, and at some point, he stole some money she had hidden in the couch, and then he was ghost.

I know Mama was embarrassed because she kept missing the potential for predatorial behavior, only looking at the fake ways these Niggas tried to help her. I don't know about any other dudes, but Errol made it clear he was trying to fuck her and me. I was amazed that she didn't realize it sooner.

Chapter Eleven

Church, Gays, and Discos

So, when I moved to Yonkers and adjusted to life in NYC's suburbs, I guess my escapism started to develop more into actions rather than just immersion in books and music.

Now, since I was older, I had more responsibility and more emotional turmoil to push down. So, I needed more ways to get away and feel free. This freedom came with 3 things – weed, women, and NYC club life. I was obsessed with all 3.

The other thing that started developing was my passion for creativity in the kitchen. Food was also my friend from way back, so I always told myself that I also love to cook since I love to eat. This was another way I tried to win Mama's approval since I got my love of food from her.

Additionally, being the chief cook in the house seemed less like a chore and more fun for me. My best friend Nick put me on how to hook up the generic box mac-n-cheese with some ground beef, Sazón, and onions, and I was amazed. From then on, I made it my mission to transform that government cheese food into culinary works of art.

I was already making recipes from all of my Mother's cookbooks, many times to her displeasure. She would say, "Why can't you make some regular food? It has too much seasoning!" She would be mad as hell that I messed up her groceries and wasted her money. Feeding four kids is expensive, even with the free shit from the government food handouts.

I was very heavy handed with the herbs and got cussed out often until I learned the delicate balance of creating the right flavors and salt. I started out using recipes from all the classic cookbooks, like The Joy of Cooking and my mother's friend Verta Mae Grosvenor's Vibration Cooking; my favorite was the Betty Crocker Cookbook—it had pictures. It's hard to make something, not ever knowing what it was supposed to look like or taste like. I was going off of pure imagination until I started using this book.

I usually never measured anything; I would go by Verta Mae's smell, look, and vibration method. I started off baking cookies and cakes and soon realized that baking was too restrictive because you always had to measure the ingredients. With food, I could vary the base recipe without disastrous results, and that is the way I cook to this day. I don't think I have followed a recipe exactly since my teenage years.

* * *

Once we were freed from Njoroge's controlling grip, Mama started going to Messiah Baptist Church down on Warburton Avenue in Yonkers. Their claim to fame was they were a prominent Black Baptist Church that had been involved in the Civil Rights Movement. Once Mama joined, she got thoroughly involved, and that meant so did we.

I was in the youth choir, attended Vacation Bible School, and basically volunteered at the church for various activities. I'll never forget the Sunday when Mama decided to join and be baptized. I had scurried up to the balcony because I had no desire to do all that; I knew damn well that my sinning days had just begun; I wasn't trying to commit to God all early and shit!

When the preacher had the altar call, where all the sinners are invited to come and tearfully give their lives to Christ, Mama was looking up at the balcony giving me the evil eye, and I was pointedly ignoring her. Once church was over, she yoked me up and informed me that I was getting baptized right along with her. I was terrified that God was going to strike the water with lightning because I had no intention of giving up the fun that I had just discovered.

Chapter Twelve

God's Voice at Messiah

As rebellious as I thought I was, I did enjoy some aspects of my time at Messiah Baptist as a teen. Good music has always moved me, and I love some good pageantry 'cause I'm dramatic like that.

I used to love the ushers' whole processional process with their white gloves and military precision turning the corners around the aisles. I used to feel such pride and regality up there singing my heart out to God in the youth choir.

Black churches know how to creatively arrange and harmonize a song. Mama had a beautiful soprano operatic voice, which we used to tease her about, but I secretly loved it. That's probably why, to this day, I love a good soprano vibrato.

On Sundays, I would zone out during praise and worship, just taking in the harmonies and letting my mind drift, before settling in for a nap during the sermon. I would sleep partly because of boredom, partly because my ADD was kicking in, and partly to distract me from my stomach grumbling.

Our family's custom was to eat a light breakfast and sit in church from 9 am to at least 2 pm, then go home to eat Sunday dinner. Lord have mercy on my hunger pains if it was Communion Sunday because then we wouldn't eat until 3:00 pm! Sometimes we had to wolf down our food, come BACK to evening service, or go sing somewhere as a guest choir. I am sure that is why I bristle at the thought of long traditional church services now. Can't I get my Word and still hit up a good Sunday brunch?

Anyway, one Sunday, I drifted off as usual. I'm not sure if I was completely asleep. Still, the next thing I remember was Deacon Jones singing his usual "Walk Around Heaven All Day" while pacing back and forth on the pulpit.

All of a sudden, he turned to look directly at me; he levitated off the pulpit and was suddenly right in front of me, singing directly to me. His voice sounded like thunder, and it resonated throughout my body like he was speaking to and through my every cell. All I could understand was, "You will serve Me."

The voice was jarring but not mean, and I literally felt and heard the voice in my whole being. I wasn't frightened, just surprised that this was happening to me, and I also got the feeling that my life was not going to follow the plans I thought I had. My spirit felt the equivalent of wanting to sprint from my body to avoid whatever task was just placed in my soul.

I opened my eyes and saw that no one had noticed anything; the preacher was still speaking, and the deacon was in his seat in front of me.

As I thought about what had just happened, I started getting really concerned that God wanted me to serve Him, like what did that mean? I was terrified at the thought that it meant that I was going to be a preacher. Like I said before, I had just discovered this life of clubs and beautiful women, and I was trying to ride out the pleasure train until at least 60 years old.

After church, I asked Mama, "What if God wants me to do something I don't want to do?"

She laughed and said, "Well you might as well be obedient because no matter what you do or how you try to avoid it, God will win because He is in control."

Then I was shook. I didn't even think of asking God directly what He meant because I really was afraid to know.

Chapter Thirteen

Curfew and the Club

When I turned 16, my senior year in high school, Mama decided to allow me a little more freedom by changing my curfew to 2 am, so, of course, I had to use that time to get into some grown folks things.

The problem was that in NYC the party doesn't get started until about 1 am. Clubs don't close until daylight. I, being the determined kid that I was, never stuck to that curfew. I swear I tried Mama's patience, but she realized that if she beat me like she wanted to, she would be in jail for child abuse or probably murder.

I had gotten a fake ID by then, and it said that I was 26, looking every bit of 16. Every weekend, I scoured the Village Voice to see what clubs were advertised and what events were going on in Manhattan. I had already figured out that I liked women, especially after messing with some of the lame-ass neighborhood guys. The common denominator with all of them, no matter the age or background, was that they all pulled their dicks out. Even the church boys.

I kept sleeping with men because I was really trying to

convince myself that what happened with Njoroge didn't make me gay. I was determined to at least try and like sex with men because I really wanted to feel "normal."

I also wanted to check out the clubs, and I didn't have a car, so my "dates" with older men served me twofold. I think Mama was really trying to push me away from the women thing, although we hadn't talked about it officially yet. She was pretty liberal when it came to sex, and she actually set me up with one of her church buddy's sons, who was 26 at the time!

I'm not sure what she thought I was gonna do with this troll. He was like 5ft, but he had a car and a job, so I agreed. Going out with him put me off dudes for a minute. He was the most uncouth, ignorant, George Jefferson walking-ass Nigga ever, with a baby dick.

Since he was clueless about what to do other than fuck, I set up a nice date for us on a Friday night. I had us go to my favorite Italian restaurant in midtown. Then we were going to hit up Bentley's, which was the Black folks' Studio 54 at the time.

When we got to the restaurant, it was like a sitcom with the faux pas and lack of restaurant etiquette. The maître d' rolled his eyes at me after the dude asked for some ice for his red wine.

I used to come to this restaurant with Aunt Isabel, so I was familiar with a few of the waitstaff. I was mortified being seen with this bamma.

At the disco, the dude didn't even know how to dance. I wasn't expecting a Soul Train dancer but, damn, at least be on the beat. That was it for me. I went home and told Mama, "Don't do me any favors. I can find my own dates."

* * *

I decided to pursue some older women and actually experience the intellectual dating scenes like in the movies. I needed stimulating conversation along with the visual attraction. I love witty banter and a beautiful mind, and these men were not giving me any of that.

Although I knew early on that I liked women, once we started attending church, and I took an interest in reading the Bible, I shockingly realized that I was the abomination that I was reading about. Not only was I fornicating, but I was committing the unpardonable sin of liking the same sex!

At first glance, I read the verse, Romans 1:26-27, meaning that since men had turned their passions towards each other, that left the women to love each other. Basically, in my mind, the men fucked up first, so what choice did I have?

However, after becoming obsessed with this whole sin thing and trying to be good because now I was "saved," I realized that God was talking about me!

Despite this realization, I still felt like God was unfair, especially after my experience. How could God expect me to embrace men after what I had been through? Surely, if all the other things I was taught about God were true, He knew exactly how I felt because He created me; therefore, I felt like I had to be true to myself in my gut.

Growing up in New York was extremely liberating

because NYC is a city that cultivates the celebration of individuality and rebellion against societal norms.

* * *

Since I knew that I was not really into the whole boy thing in my senior year, and I was not into the whole school dance thing, I was most definitely a jaded teen. I had decided not to attend prom. I wanted to wear a modified tuxedo like Cher, and I knew Mama wasn't going for that, so I decided to sit this one out.

She convinced me that this was a memory that I didn't want to miss, so she got our neighbor to make me a custom dress complete with a bowtie and cummerbund. Mama made me a tuxedo dress. I told her often how this was the best and most thoughtful thing she ever did for me. I felt like she really saw me and understood my androgynous inclinations.

We still had never spoken officially about me being gay. I know she knew but was hoping for a change. She did constantly mention how all my male friends were pretty and a bit feminine. I would always deny and defend them, partly because I wasn't sure what they were doing.

Anyway, I finally graduated from high school at 16 and was accepted into the Urban Legal Studies program at CCNY in Harlem. It was an accelerated law program where you combined undergrad and law school. The curriculum focused on civil rights law and issues affecting underserved communities. I was used to being one of the smartest in the room, and now I went from being special to drowning in the real world of academia.

Out of the 35 students in the class, only 2 of us were straight out of high school. This program attracted people that may have already worked in the legal field or, at the very least, were old enough to have experienced firsthand the historical events being discussed in class. I was also used to not having to put in any real studying to get my As, so this was entirely new. Like I had to do REAL work, and my brain went into escape mode. I decided to pursue some power in practicing witchcraft and indulge my newfound love of clubs by trying to go every night if I could.

Anything to not deal with the fact that I didn't think I was really good enough to make it as a lawyer. Although I was book smart, my emotional maturity level was in elementary school at that time, and it derailed me a little bit more. I basically flunked out of every class that semester by partying, and the one class I did pass was not by my own efforts.

* * *

So, I had decided to explore the world of witchcraft after reading books on how to cast various benign spells. I heard about this seal and saint that you pray to for good grades, and I figured I could use all the help I could get since I hadn't been to class basically all semester.

I went to the Botanica, which is a Latin spiritual shop. I purchased a seal that I had to wear on my chest after saying a prayer, and then I took my Greek Mythology final. Despite having only attended orientation for this class, I passed the final exam with an 'A' to my complete surprise. I figured I was on to something, and I decided to go further.

In my first year in college, I embraced the freedom of living in NYC and celebrating my gayness. I used to scour the Village Voice newspaper for club ads and festivals that I could spend my weekends at. I discovered this one little gay club in the West Village called Tory's that had $10 all you could drink every Friday night, and they were lax with the IDs.

While working at my McDonald's job, I discovered that basically all of the management was gay and quite willing to fraternize. My boy Nick and I convinced our managers Joe and Miriam to drive into the city to hang at Tory's. I had no idea that Miriam liked me, and I was clueless that Joe was crushing on my boy.

Miriam was this stocky Cuban butch with a cute face. I wasn't particularly attracted to her, but once we got to the club, she started acting like we were together, and since she drove, I went along with it. I was more curious than anything else.

I wanted to practice my moves that I had been fantasizing for years, so when I met someone I really wanted to impress, I would know what I was doing. Sometime that night, after being a few drinks in, we ended up in the bathroom stall, tonguing each other down.

When I came back out, Nicky looked at me all shocked like, wow, you really just kissed your first girl. Of course, I started plotting a way to take it all the way there. It was a challenge because she was really into the butch role and not used to letting women make love to her.

She had a longtime wifey by the way, which I knew about but really didn't care because she was just a means to an end for me. I knew I wanted to be the dominant one in the situation, and it was such an ego stroker for me to flip her over.

The first time I went down on a woman, I knew why men went so crazy over women, and I felt right at home in it. I couldn't get enough of it. I was basically obsessed with women after that experience.

The Player was unleashed...

Chapter Fourteen

Mr. J

So, after we fled the Bronx and moved to Yonkers, Mama went through an ugly custody battle with Njoroge. For some reason, because she was so damn naïve, Mama thought that, although Njoroge was a rapist, he was still my siblings' biological father and he should continue to have a relationship with them.

That was the biggest mistake she ever made because Njoroge picked them up one weekend and kidnapped them for about a year.

According to the law, whoever has physical custody of the children can keep them until the court proceedings are completely settled. My baby brother was staying with my evil Auntie in Queens still because he was safe there. Njoroge was too afraid of Auntie D to even darken her doorstep.

Mama had to take an additional night job doing medical transcription to pay for the lawyer's fees to get her kids back. After all of that, Njoroge was granted visitation rights, but he was not supposed to come to our house or even know where we lived.

* * *

Once all the custody stuff was over, Mama started dating again, and this time she met Mr. J. I came home from school one day, and he was in the living room, putting together some bunk beds for my brothers. Mama was grinning like a Cheshire cat, and I knew then Mr. J was going to be around for a while.

I was not into him at all; of course, I was still leery from all of her other poor choices of men, and this one didn't seem much better since I could smell the alcohol seeping from his pores in the middle of the afternoon! I immediately was plotting to get rid of him.

Mama had other plans, though. Mr. J was a big strapping Southern man from St. George, South Carolina, and he displayed that Southern charm with a bit of Sagittarian swag and regaled Mama with his stories of his family down South.

Their real connection was the food and the partying. Mr. J could throw down in the kitchen and probably in other areas too. Mr. J came along at the right time when Mama was the most vulnerable and needed a protector.

He stepped in and contributed financially to the household, and he was neither a wife-beater nor a molester. I couldn't appreciate him at the time, but as I got older, I realized he was a good dude, and he really didn't have to take on Mama and her 4 kids.

Well, one Saturday morning, Mama and Mr. Jim left to go on a bus trip to Atlantic City and left me home to babysit. I was on punishment for running up the phone bill, so Mama had placed a lock on the phone. I was on the phone in the bedroom yakking it up with one of my buddies; I had her call me when suddenly I heard a loud banging on the front door.

Then, I heard my sister and brother say, "Daddy!!" and I sprinted out of that room like Usain Bolt. I ran to the door and slammed it shut just as they were about to let Njoroge into the apartment. I was terrified! He was never supposed to come to our house, and I couldn't even call the police because the phone was locked!

It was so chaotic with the kids screaming to let him in and him yelling at me to open the door. I ran back to the bedroom and used a lighter to burn the lock off the phone, so I could call 911. When I ran back to the door, the kids had opened it again, and he was trying to force his way in, although the chain was on the door. I pushed my weight against the door, but he was much stronger than me, so I didn't know how long I could hold him off.

As I was pushing the door, suddenly, Njoroge was yanked back from behind, and I heard him getting punched. Mr. J and Mama had returned unexpectedly from the bus trip and caught Njoroge trying to get in the house.

She later told me that God told her to get back to the house because we were in danger. Mr. J beat that Nigga down and then came back to the house to get me.

He gave me a huge hunting knife and asked me if I wanted to go get Njoroge. I was like, "Hell, yeah," and off we went running down Locust Hill to whip some ass.

That was the first time in my life I had a real protector, other than my Granny. Although I still didn't trust him fully, he won points with me that day.

Chapter Fifteen

Oh Shit, I'm Really Gay

So, although I couldn't handle college freshman year's academic responsibility, I excelled at developing a work ethic and embracing my newfound sexuality. I always kept a job, and at school, I spent most of my time clowning and watching the boys queen out and vogue in the common area.

I even advocated for the LGBT students to have their own exclusive club time, just like every other social club at school. I was really taken in and accepted by the gays, and it felt like I had found my tribe. I also figured out really quickly how segregated the gay community is when it came to partying.

I loved dancing with my folks at Tory's, but I wondered where the Black gay folks were. Normally, my boy and I were the only Blacks at the clubs we went to. At the time, one of my best friends, Jill, had an older brother who was gay, and he offered to take me to the infamous Black gay club, Better Days, down in Midtown Manhattan.

From the time we stepped in the club – the fashions, the pageantry, and all the butches and queens all comfortable in their own skin and twirling to their heart's content – I was at home! This vibe is what I had been looking for. I wanted to learn about the culture from a Black perspective.

* * *

To make it even better, Mama always compared me to other teen girls at church and asked me why I couldn't be more like them. To my hilarious surprise, the one girl that Mama used to praise because she was the only one besides myself that didn't get pregnant in the church, was perched upon the barstool in her big butch girlfriend's arms!

Man, I couldn't wait to tell my mother what I witnessed. I guess I was more like her than she thought. It was even more satisfying to me as she was the deacon's daughter, the same deacon that tried to chastise me publicly after church for going to a choir rehearsal of the Yonkers Community Choir, which was known to be mostly gay.

I made sure I let him know where I saw his precious daughter, right up in the gay club. I was appalled at the hypocrisy of both the deacon and my pastor's wife, who also tried to embarrass me after church. She had the nerve to ask me why I defied the pastor's instructions to stay away from that choir.

I was like, "First of all, my mother gave me her permission to go. She would rather me be at a choir rehearsal on a Friday night instead of worrying about me being up in the club somewhere in the city. Furthermore, half of our choir, including the directors chosen by the pastor, were flaming queens." I had to check my tongue because I was so close to cussing out the woman of God right in the sanctuary.

But Mama backed me up all the way. I think she was taken aback by them trying to do her parenting job too. She had already observed how corrupt the church leadership was when she was a Trustee. Mama told me how she left that position because she witnessed all the trustees taking money from the collection and stuffing their pockets while counting it.

Mama didn't play with God, and she wanted no part of that shit. After that incident, we basically were involved with the church to give us extracurricular activities, but I don't think she respected the pastor anymore.

* * *

During all of this sexual exploration, I was still desperately trying to deny that I solely liked women. I started messing with two of the security guards at the college and quickly found out that guys do gossip.

I naïvely thought with my 16-year-old brain that this 26-year-old fine-ass Guyanese dude was my boyfriend. I took the train all the way over to his spot in the Bronx damn near every weekday, and I even brought him food sometimes.

After a few weeks, he mentioned that he had talked to the other security guard that I slept with, and I knew that I was basically being viewed as a whore. After that experience, I recognized the importance of being respected by whomever I slept with and never to source dick from the same pool. From then on, I was extra careful to do my dirt by my lonesome and made sure none of my pieces knew each other.

* * *

I finally had to have the "I'm coming out" conversation with Mama, and I was so confused by her reaction. All through high school, Mama would accuse me of being a "bull dagger," and I would vehemently deny it, but I got tired of lying when I got to college.

One day after I had interrogated her about the message a girl I was crushing on left for me, I finally relented and said, "Yes, I am gay." She actually told me that she was disappointed in me, and I should have known better! I told her that was the most ignorant thing she ever said to me at the risk of being slapped.

Up until that point, I figured she knew but was waiting for me to confirm it. Plus, if there was ever any reason for someone to "turn gay," I figured rape being my first sexual experience was it. She knew better than anyone the abuse I suffered, and she still thought that I should be with men?

Also, her hypocrisy was blatant. All my life, Mama had gay friends. She even told me how her favorite cousin growing up in Trinidad was gay and eventually moved to Canada to be out freely. She clearly accepted her friends being gay, but not her child.

I was crushed but adamant that I was sticking with the lesbian thing. I could smoke weed, have sex with older men, and drink liquor at the age of 16, but I couldn't be a lesbian. I decided then that I was going to live out despite what anyone thought. I knew that God knew what I liked. If I was going to have to answer for all the other grimy shit I did, being deceptive about my sexuality was not going to be one of them. However, the weight of her words seeped in that day. The roots of shame were pushed deeper in.

* * *

After I flunked out of freshman year and lost all my financial aid and scholarship money, I had to figure out what to do with my life at 17. I also figured out that fast food could not be my future. I had gotten a job at Roy Rogers down by the Empire State Building, although I lived in Yonkers, and it only paid minimum wage.

The most impractical job decision ever. I was closing up one night, and we were robbed at gunpoint, and I knew that this life was not going to work for me. Ever since I had scored the top score on the ASVAB test to get into the armed services, the recruiters had been circling and trying to convince Mama to sign me up.

I originally had no intention of joining the service; patriotism was far from my mind, but it was a way to get out of class, so I took the test.

Also, Mr. J, who was around permanently by then, convinced Mama that this was the best solution for me since it had worked so well for him. The Army recruiter was the most persistent, so that's who I finally went with.

He explained all the college money and lifelong benefits. What especially interested me was the career paths I could take. It was peacetime, and there was no immediate threat of war, so I figured I was safe.

I was going to travel the world, get a career, and get paid for all of it. Since I was only 17 years old, Mama had to sign off on my induction at the recruiter's office. When he asked the two dreaded questions: Do you smoke weed? Are you a homosexual? Mama gave me the death stare, and I knew that I better give the right answer. I admitted to the weed but promised to be clean by the piss test, and I outright denied the gayness.

Again, I could be a weed smoker and be trained to kill people, but I couldn't love the same sex. Let that sink in.

Part Two

I'm In the Army Now

My ASVAB score was high enough to land a medical job, which according to my recruiter, was one of the most coveted positions in the military because it directly transferred to civilian careers once you left the Army.

I signed up to become a Pharmacy Specialist and volunteered to serve for 4 years. My preference was to be stationed overseas. I did that just to spite my mother since she wanted me gone so badly.

I always suspected that Mr. J was in her ear about getting me out of the house. He was always trying to set me up for her wrath by acting like he was cool with me and bringing me weed, but then telling Mama I had weed in the house. I hated that snitch shit.

All the brownie points he had gotten from me for protecting me from Njoroge were lost. I would outsmart him, though, by giving the weed to my boy's mom, who was an avid smoker.

My sister told me years later that Mr. J lied about being in the Army. I was so done that, once again, Mama was fooled by her choice of a man. Despite how I ended up in the Army, that was the best decision I ever made because it started my road to real independence and emotional maturity. It also jumpstarted my years of endless sexcapades on several continents.

* * *

The Army recruiter had been harassing me since my senior year when I scored highly on the ASVAB test. I had no idea what I was doing on that test; I simply was doing it to get out of class that day.

Anyway, I had absolutely no intention of joining the Army because patriotism was not in my blood, not as the child of immigrants and well aware of racism being practiced in America. However, after a few days of Mama ranting about me not being a grown woman staying in her house, my impulsiveness kicked in, and I agreed to meet with the recruiter.

Now, had I known the difference in each Armed Service's reputation, I probably would have gone with the Air Force. The AF career choices were wider. The bases and duty stations were located in places that I wanted to visit, at least overseas. So, the Army is smart; just like any other organization out to recruit poor people to their way of life, they send their most charismatic salespeople to the hood to spit their game.

In my case, patriotism had very little to do with my decision to sign up, and it was more about economic survival. Once the Black recruiter spun the tale of how the Army would train me for a career, provide salary, housing, and health and education benefits while sending me to exotic lands where I could frolic as I pleased, I was intrigued.

He emphasized how, in the Army, they don't see race, only green. He sealed the deal by reminding me that we were in peacetime and there was no war on the horizon, so my enlistment would be at the most ideal time. Of course, Mama was hooked and kept giving me the evil eye, so I agreed to enlist.

Once I agreed, then came the questions about my lifestyle, the weed, and the women. Back when I enlisted in the summer of 1984, it was illegal to be gay in the armed services, with the penalty of jail and a dishonorable discharge. I denied everything, and I even did the Bill Clinton thing where I admitted to smoking but didn't inhale, all while Mama was giving me the death stare, like "You better not fuck this up!"

Once I realized that I had just signed my life away for the next 4 years, I wanted to go overseas to get the complete experience. Since I was still only 17, Mama gladly signed the papers to allow me to enlist and get out of NYC to start a new path in life. I think she also thought that by getting out of NY, I would chill with the women since I wouldn't be openly able to live that life. I soon found out that I jumped from the frying pan straight into the lesbian fire baby!

Things were looking up...

Chapter Sixteen

Basic Training

It was very evident from the organized confusion of our trip to Ft. Jackson, South Carolina that this was going to be an exercise in mind games and brainwashing for the next 8 weeks of my life.

First of all, we were literally herded into cattle trucks and driven from the Basic Training reception station at zero dark thirty hours. In military time, it means the middle of the damn night, like 2:00 am, to another reception station to be issued our soldier essentials.

The night before, we had been bussed from the airport to the reception station and assigned bunks and basically introduced to the other recruits we would be in Basic Training with. There were girls and women of all ages and backgrounds from pretty much every state and territory, all of us clueless about what was about to go down.

The first person that I met was this big ebony-skinned dyke who used to be a corrections officer at Rikers Island, and she was leering at me like a fox in a chicken coop. I knew she lied on her application, too, because I was sure she thought I would be her snack.

Meanwhile, I had my eye on this girl straight from Puerto Rico named Zulma Reyes. She was petite with gorgeous, sun-kissed skin, big brown eyes with long naturally luscious lashes, perfectly feathered raven hair, and spoke so sweetly with that sexy accent. I decided that she would be my buddy; no matter who they assigned me to, I was sticking close to her.

When we were jolted awake by the drill sergeants in the middle of the night, she was so disoriented that she fell out of the bunk bed and started speaking in Spanish. Since I was halfway fluent in Spanish back then, I spoke to her in Spanish and calmed her down. After that, she became my buddy for real; I was kind of her protector.

Sort of like in prison, where you choose your "prison bae" or they choose you. Since she was so fine, all the butch ones were coming for her, and I made it my personal mission to be her official bodyguard.

* * *

My thoughts during that cattle truck ride with the smell of the red clay dirt and the blistering South Carolina heat was: this is what the slaves had to endure daily. I was terrified because I had no idea what to expect, but I kept telling myself, thousands of other people got through this, and so could I.

My only comfort came from knowing that the drill sergeants couldn't physically touch you, and they couldn't directly curse you out. The brainwashing started almost immediately with the drill sergeants yelling at us and trying to instill fear and confusion to sort of break down your psyche so they could retrain it with Army propaganda. I refused to let anyone see me fearful or weak, so I set my NYC stone face in full effect. I refused to be broken.

The drill sergeants do erase your individuality by emphasizing rank and only referring to you by your surname. Then you're inundated with how the Army is the best thing to happen to you because ain't nothing out there "on the block."

By the time you graduate from Basic, you wonder how the rest of the world operates in such chaos and disorder. We were also told that we were now the US government's property, and we no longer even had control of our bodies or thoughts.

We had to memorize endless regulations and perform tasks with precision within minimal amounts of time. I had to unlearn my healthy NY bred distrust of people and implicitly trust my superiors' commands without question.

My pride took a hit because I sure wasn't in the habit of taking orders on account of my naturally rebellious nature. The main reasons I stuck it out were the threat of jail and the fact that I really had nothing to go back "home" to in NYC. I had been kicked out of the nest officially, and I had to keep that reality in the forefront of my mind.

Although everyone had these fantastic stories of how great their lives were "back on the block," the reality was that we were all there to improve our lives in some way and failure was not an option.

* * *

My assigned platoon buddy was Diehl, a wiry little white girl from West Virginia, who was also 17 and was in the Army to make a way to rescue her little sister from her abusive drunken father. She was so determined to finish that she trained through a broken foot before finally being forced to take a break in the 4th week. I was heartbroken for her. She was literally using the Army to save her sister's life, and now it was going to be delayed.

We also had Durant, a 34-year-old sister from Chicago who joined at the top of the age limit because she had a mother and son to care for and needed the benefits. She struggled because at that age, it's challenging to take barked orders from people younger than you and not slap the shit outta them for being disrespectful.

Then, I met the many Midwestern girls who had never seen a real-life Black person, and they all were fascinated with my hair. A few Southern redneck girls were probably racist AF before dealing with this situation, where most of their superiors were Black. Despite all of our differences, we formed a camaraderie that made us want the whole platoon to succeed.

* * *

The Army instills the idea of sticking together as a unit; if one fails, we all fail, and so we got into the habit of having group prayer and encouraging one another every night before lights out. There are a few major tasks that you must master to graduate from Basic; the gas chamber, the gun range, the grenade range, and passing a Physical Training test.

In addition to this, you had to know the code of conduct by heart and assemble and disassemble an M16 rifle in 2 minutes. As a matter of fact, you had to do most things in 2 minutes, like take a shower and eat. To this day, I am still amazed at what can be done in a mere 2 minutes.

Anyway, when it came down to the tasks, this is where the victorious were separated from the quitters. This is where I had to push myself to shine and give myself no excuses. We had to run 2 miles every morning before breakfast. If you fell behind, your buddy had to stay behind and run with you, ultimately delaying breakfast for the whole platoon.

I remember being so determined not to fall behind on my run that I threw up as I reached the finish line, but I made it. I had a few moments like that, where I physically pushed my body's limits and learned to control my mind to ignore discomfort and complete a task. I learned how to zone out and visualize scenes in my mind during those 20-mile road marches. I found that I liked the discipline and order because I had no idea it was in me. I loved having my living area be meticulously clean without the threat of roaches.

I took such pride in being inspected and told that my uniform and boots were "squared away." This was my validation. I had now found a form of validation outside of academics, and I guess it helped me find pride in myself again.

* * *

This was also where I know I received some supernatural intervention from humans and angels. So, my first challenge came at the firearm range because my eyesight isn't the best. Those government-issued Rape Prevention Glasses, our nickname for those Godawful horn-rimmed black glasses, were barely adequate.

I had my first encounter with Drill Sergeant Owens at the range as well. She was my mentor/stalker during my whole Basic Training experience. Although she wasn't my platoon sergeant, she took me under her wing, and I am sure if I was in her platoon, there would have been some fraternizing going on.

While we were all in formation walking to the range, she called me over to her, and I had to stand at attention while she looked me up and down. She asked me my first name, a form of flirting, because we strictly went by last names in the Army.

She made it quite obvious she was attracted to me, and if I could have turned colors, I would have been beet red. She stood face to face with me, so close the brim of her hat touched mine, and scowled, then told me to drop and do some pushups. She made up some minor infraction that warranted that punishment, and then she calmly told me she would be watching me.

I was so embarrassed, but she was fine and a higher rank, so I let it go. I am not usually attracted to aggressive women. Still, her crisp uniform, cinnamon colored skin, gorgeous smile, and that raspy Southern twang was so damn sexy to me. I even liked how her Jheri curls were poppin'. Yeah, it was the 80s, so Jheri curls were standard for the Black soldiers, even me. For the duration of Basic Training, Drill

Sergeant Owens made sure she was there while I was completing each major task required.

That first day at the range, I struggled with hitting my targets because I couldn't see them clearly. I also had to practice resisting the rifle's kickback and master the prone position, where you lie on the ground and shoot.

Shooting a rifle is nothing like that bullshit on TV; if you're unprepared, that kickback can take out your shoulder. Drill Sergeant Owens actually came and lay down on top of me to demonstrate the proper prone position to further embarrass me. I was so mortified because I could do nothing but lie there and take it. If she had been a guy, it would clearly have been sexual assault.

After her assistance, I did become a better shot, though. Anyway, about 3 of us failed to qualify as accurate marksmen, so we had to pass a final test or risk not graduating on time. That night, both floors of women got together for group prayer, and we asked God to help us on that range the next day. The next day, as I still struggled with seeing the targets clearly, I was amazed that a second after I released my bullet, the targets kept falling. I knew it wasn't my aim because I would miss a shot only 50 meters away, but I hit every shot that was 250 meters away.

To this day, I figured it was a result of that group prayer or a really benevolent training sergeant who manipulated the targets to our advantage. Still, all of us advanced to the next task as proficient shooters.

* * *

The next major test was to throw a live hand grenade over a wall without blowing everyone up. This was a test of speed and strength because you only had seconds to find shelter after the grenade pin was released and launched into the air; hopefully, it would clear the 15-foot wall and land the grenade in the safe zone.

Welp, one of the ladies in our platoon threw the weakest underhand spaghetti arm throw, and we all looked in horror as the grenade hit the wall and rolled back toward us. The drill sergeants screamed, "GET DOWN, GET DOWN!" and I only had time to flatten myself to the ground and press my face in the dirt with my helmet shielding my face before the grenade exploded with a deafening roar.

When I lifted my head, all I saw was shrapnel and blood from where the one drill sergeant hadn't fully made it to shelter because he was ensuring all of the trainees were safe. I was traumatized, doubly so, because the sergeant that got injured was a fine brother and one of the nicer cadre.

After that incident, we all cussed her out for being lazy and endangering everyone. She was put out for mental health issues. A couple of women were put out for mental issues, like the one that pushed another recruit down a flight of stairs and spit on the drill sergeants because they yelled at her.

Anyway, by supernatural grace, all of us went back to the barracks unscathed. The lesson I came away with was that not giving your best can sometimes be a matter of life or death. The private with the weak throw had developed a reputation for giving up and throwing crying tantrums instead of pushing herself like most of us. That one time she didn't even try cost her an opportunity to change her life.

* * *

The next test was to climb up a 50-foot wall and successfully rappel down. That high up, I might as well have been jumping out of an airplane; I was terrified.

But here came my guardian angel again, Drill Sergeant Owens. She said, "Now private, you gotta be careful coming down that rope, you gotta protect the kitty, you don't want to burn that up now, do you?" She proceeded to show me how to adjust my uniform and hands so the rope would not burn my groin during the descent to the ground.

I thought she was just being extra attentive and trying to flirt until I saw the rope burns and ripped uniform suffered by the girl that went in front of me, without that special set of instructions.

* * *

The final test was the physical training test, where we had to do pushups and sit-ups and run 2 miles in less than 20 minutes. After all of my smart-ass retorts and subsequent punishments throughout Basic, I was well versed in knocking out pushups and sit-ups, but that run though....

I absolutely hated running and really pushed myself to finish during our daily, sometimes 10-mile runs. I must have looked like I was about to fall out, and the next thing I knew, Drill Sergeant Owens trotted up next to me and ran with me around the track for the final mile.

She kept calling me Wanjiru and saying, "You got this,

you got this, only a little bit more," encouraging me all the way until I crossed the finish line just under the time limit.

Completing Basic Training was exhilarating because it was the first time I completed something that was not academic and completely out of my comfort zone. I also recognized that I had favor on my life judging from the supernatural help that I received.

I left Basic with a sense of pride, a banging body, and a budding cigarette addiction. I picked up smoking because I learned quickly that only smokers got breaks throughout the day during training.

* * *

My next stop was San Antonio, Texas to train as a pharmacy tech, but that didn't last long, much to my disappointment. My pharmacy assistant training was supposed to be a year long, but it didn't take but 5 weeks for me to flunk out of the chemistry portion.

Science was never my strong point, and I figured that they would just let me choose another medical profession, but that wasn't how the Army job thing worked. Apparently, you could only choose from the available jobs listed on the day you went to be assigned a new job. I wanted to be assigned a psychology job, but instead, combat telecommunications specialist was the only job available that day.

While waiting to be shipped off to my new training site in Ft. Gordon, August, Georgia, I got my first chance to hit the gay club in San Antonio. The thing about being gay in the service was that it was like a secret society.

At every duty station, we would find each other and support one another. We called each other "family," and my first buddy was Tony Garces, a 5 foot 3 inch Mexican queen that I met in the mess hall. He swished so hard that I couldn't believe no one knew he was gay!

Anyway, he and I decided to sneak off base to hit the club in our dress green uniform since we weren't allowed to wear civilian clothes yet. We successfully made it out of the main gate and strolled down to a nearby hotel to change into our club clothes. Once we got into the club and checked out the scene, it was like we were home.

I was enthralled by the beautiful, petite Mexican drag queens, and the music was thumping, so we danced all night, enjoying our first taste of freedom in months. As I was twirling and flinging my Jheri curl juice across the floor, I happened to look across the dance floor, and, to my horror, there was one of my instructors, SFC Rios. We spotted each other simultaneously, and before I could react by running out of there, she winked at me and motioned me over to her.

I figured I was busted, so I might as well talk to her. It turned out she was more scared I would tell someone than I was concerned about her. She bought me a drink, and we swore each other to secrecy; then, in true cougar fashion, she planted a kiss on me, winked again, and walked away. I didn't mind because she was a sexy, doe-eyed, thick caramel-skinned, petite, gorgeous, high-ranking Latina sergeant, who I already had a slight crush on anyway.

I continued to party my weekends away unbothered until I was shipped off to redneck-ass Augusta, Georgia for my telecom training. I couldn't wait to finish there and move on to my next duty station in Germany. Augusta was a lot less minority friendly than San Antonio. After my first and only visit to the one lonely lesbian club, I was content to leave Augusta unexplored.

* * *

I was shipped off to Nuremberg, Germany in May 1985 to begin my 2-year deployment. Before being stationed there, I had absolutely no desire to visit any part of West Germany.

It was still West Germany because the Berlin Wall had not yet come down. All I knew about Germany was the history of Hitler.

Still, I had heard from other Black soldiers that Europeans love Black people, so I didn't actually dread the prospect of living there. I was 18 years old, my first time living on my own (sort of, it was still a barracks) on a whole other continent and no idea what to expect from Army life.

While I was waiting in the USO lounge at the airport on my way to Germany, I ran into the hip hop group Run DMC, who was my favorite at the time. They told me they were on their way to do a concert at some base in Germany, and I was elated to know that I could at least experience some of my culture while stationed there.

I took that celebrity sighting as a good sign that Germany might turn out to be all right. I was off to my new adventure courtesy of the US government, and my life was looking up.

Book 2 coming in early 2022.

About the Author

Colyn Wanjiru is a blogger and soon to be bestselling author who writes about the intersection of faith, supernatural experiences and spiritual growth learned through her life experiences. She is a first generation Trinidadian American, native New Yorker, foodie, cannabis connoisseur, wellness entrepreneur, hip hop fanatic, reiki healer and a Christ representer. Colyn stepped out on faith and left a decades long lucrative career in telecom to pursue a career more suited to her passions of writing, cooking and holistic wellness. Her book, "Memoirs of a Former Bitter Bitch, Pt 1", is the first in a series chronicling the stories and lessons she has learned while pursuing her own healing. She currently resides in Maryland while waiting for God to show her the next leg of this life's adventure.

Made in United States
North Haven, CT
13 April 2022

18215240R00078